A-LEVEL YEAR 1 SOCIOLOGY FOR OCR

UNIT 1B (Youth Subcultures)

SOCIOLOGY 1B2 STUDY GUIDE

Published independently by Tinderspark Press
© Jonathan Rowe 2021
www.psychologywizard.net
www.philosophydungeon.weebly.com

CONTENTS

ABOUT THIS BOOK

This book offers advice for teachers and students approaching OCR A-Level Sociology, **Paper 1 Section B2 (Youth Subcultures)**.

Study Guides for **Papers 2** and **3** will follow.

Paper 1 Section B (Option 2)

This covers about two thirds of **Paper 1** in OCR Sociology. There are 3 questions worth 52 marks out of the 90 marks for the entire paper. It should take candidates 55-60 minutes to complete.

This is quite a slim study guide for such a big part of the exam!

The reason for this is that the Guide for **1A (Socialisation, Culture & Identity)** has already introduced the foundational concepts that candidates will use throughout the rest of their Sociology A-Level. Some of that material is reiterated here.

Perspectives

Candidates who have completed Study Guide 1A will be familiar with **Functionalism, Marxism, Feminism** and **Interactionism**. This Guide explores Neo-Marxism in more depth and introduces **Postmodernism** and the **New Right. Weberianism** will be introduced in the future Study Guide for **2B (Inequality)**.

Functionalism is, strictly speaking, an obsolete theory in Sociology, but its ideas remain very influential in politics and in the media. Even though students who move onto a degree-level study of Sociology at university will find that Functionalism barely features, it is presented here as a theoretical perspective that is both intellectually and morally equivalent to the 'conflict' perspectives of Marxism and Feminism. The aim is to help students evaluate sociological arguments from any point of view.

Studies

Sociological 'studies' (for A-Level purposes) are often papers published in academic journals, but are sometimes magazine articles, pamphlets produced by charities or activists or popular books.

Where texts are particularly famous or influential, I offer their names, but candidates are not expected to know the names of studies in the exam. All the studies referenced in this Study Guide are brought together at the end in a revision aid (p71).

YOUTH SUBCULTURES: CONTENT

What's this topic about?

This introduces you to the main sociological theories about Youth, in particular why YOUTH SUBCULTURES form and the appeal of DEVIANT SUBCULTURES for the young.

This should help you answer some important questions:

- What is Youth in society: is it a good thing or a period of stress and danger? Is youth culture significant in society or are young people exploited and marginalised?

- Why is there youth deviance: is it natural for young people to break the rules or are they vulnerable to dangerous pressures? Is society growing more dangerous for the young or are they too coddled from reality?

- What role does the Media play in the lives of young people: is it empowering them, corrupting them or misrepresenting them?

Youth

Like other animals, humans experience biological MATURATION. They mature into adults, gaining size, strength and physical and mental skills but also reproductive characteristics. Puberty is particularly important as a visible indicator of maturation, although maturation continues through the teens and into adulthood.

In many traditional societies, the transition from child to adult is marked by a **rite of passage**, which is usually a religious ceremony and might be accompanied by a test (such as, to hunt an animal). After that, the former child is considered an adult.

'Youth' is an alternative to the institution of a rite of passage. The young person has some adult privileges (staying out late, buying their own clothes, not requiring supervision at all times) but in other ways is still in a childlike state (prevented from joining in many adult activities, like drinking alcohol, working full time or engaging in sex). Youth is a period of training and preparation for adult life.

Because Youth isn't fixed by biology, it is **socially constructed**. Different cultures view Youth starting or ending at different times. For example, you are not considered **criminally responsible** until you are 15 in Sweden, but 6 in North Carolina, USA. The **'age of majority'** (when you are legally allowed to participate in adult activities) is 18 in the UK, but 20 in Japan and 21 in Mississippi, USA.

People have different views on Youth. Some wish to see the age extended, arguing that young people are still not mature enough at 18 or even 21 to handle society's many demands. Others wish to remove it, arguing that young people are being denied their rights and freedoms – for example, to vote on matters that concern them.

CHAPTER ONE – YOUTH CULTURE

Culture means the things that are shared by a group that mark it out as distinctive. For most of history and in most societies, there was no such thing as 'Youth Culture' because young people weren't a distinctive group. At the start of the 19th century, children started work in factories or in mines at age 10 and joined the Navy at age 12. In other words, as soon as children could function as adults, they did so, and took part in the adult working culture.

As the Industrial Revolution progressed, the idea of children working in dangerous conditions became distasteful to Victorians. UK laws made it compulsory to stay in school till 10, then until 12. At the end of the Second World War, in 1946, the UK school leaving age was raised to 15. Today, it is 18.

Most historians trace the emergence of a distinctive **Youth Culture** to the 1950s and '60s, when young people were not allowed to join the adult world of work but had enough money and independence to interact in society away from home. This Youth Culture expressed itself in distinctive youth fashions and enjoyment of new 'pop' music, new dancing styles and new leisure pastimes.

Right from the beginning, there was a concern that Youth was a period of *'Sturm und Drang'* (*'storm & stress'* according to **G. Stanley Hall, 1904)** where hormones produced out-of-control behaviour. This biological view of Youth takes the Nature side in the **Nature-Nurture Debate**.

Research: the pop music of the 1950s, especially rock & roll (and Elvis Presley!) but also skiffle and jazz; the youth fashions of the '50s in hair and dress; the significance of motor bikes and scooters; the rise of vinyl LPs and the pop charts; pirate radio; dance halls; movies aimed at young people (especially horror, science fiction); boys and girls comics of the '50s and '60s

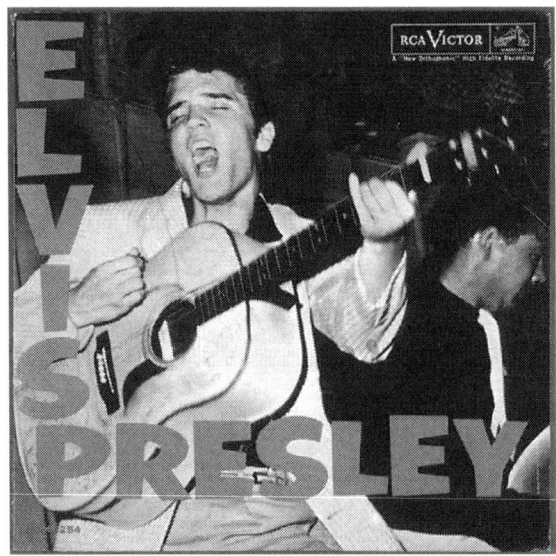

Elvis Presley defined Youth Culture in the 1950s

Positive Views of Youth Culture

Youth Culture is often praised for its novelty, energy and creativity. Youth Culture generates new fashions, new language in the form of youth slang, new art and new ideas. It often leads the way in protesting injustice and demanding a better future. Whether it's the music of the Beatles or the environmental idealism of Greta Thunberg, new ideas from Youth Culture move into the mainstream culture and change it for the better. It helps society progress.

Youth Culture also benefits young people themselves. Life in 21st century societies is complicated and important decisions have to be made about relationships, lifestyles and careers. Are you straight or gay? Do you take recreational drugs? Do you want to go to university? It's difficult to un-do many of these decisions later and the consequences can be far-reaching. Youth Culture offers a period of experimentation when adolescents can 'try out' some options, make mistakes, break the rules and then 'put it behind them' and move forward.

Negative Views of Youth Culture

Traditionally, Youth Culture was viewed as *'Sturm und Drang'* and linked to out-of-control hormones.

Youth Culture isn't always fresh and spontaneous. It's also a type of **Consumer** and young people are a target for big corporations wanting to sell them things: high sugar sweets and snacks packed with additives, violent video games, music glamorising crime, porn. Youth Culture is **exploitational** and often carries very bad messages about lifestyle and morals.

Similarly, Youth Culture doesn't benefit society as a whole if young people are being **socialised** into a selfish mindset that only cares about appearances and pleasure.

Some worry that Youth Culture is reaching younger children, introducing them to sexual content, bad language and normalising drug-taking or violence when they're too young to understand it properly. Others worry that Youth Culture is extending later into life, so that young people don't 'grow out of it' in their 20s or 30s. This leads to **'Kidults'** who are grown men and women still chasing a lifestyle of drugs, video games and casual sex when they ought to be settling down with families and careers.

RESEARCH PROFILE: MEAD (1928)

Margaret Mead (1901-1978) visited Samoa in the 1920s. Samoa is an island group in the Pacific and, in the early 20th century, the inhabitants had little contact with the outside world. Mead described her findings in *Coming of Age in Samoa* (1928) after studying 68 girls (aged 9-20) from three villages on the island of Ta'ū., especially the village of Fitiuta. Mead learned the Samoan language and used a sociological method called ethnography to observe and record the behaviour of the Samoan girls.

Mead's research challenges the idea that adolescence is necessarily a period of **Sturm und Drang** ('Storm and Stress') because of the biological changes occurring around puberty. Against this strongly Nature-view, Mead argues for a **social constructivist** view that the Samoan girls made the transition to adulthood without 'storm & stress' for three reasons:

Diffusion of responsibility: Children were raised by the whole community rather than just the two parents. This reduced the need for adolescents to rebel against their parents.

Openness: Children were not shielded from death, sex or suffering. Mead describes children watching childbirth happen, including miscarriages.

Sexual freedom: Adolescents were allowed to experiment with sex, including masturbation and homosexuality, without being judged or stigmatised

Mead argues that American culture at that time was confusing and oppressive compared to the carefree culture of Samoa. Mead complains about the conflicting messages American adolescents receive: *"our children are faced with half a dozen standards of morality: a double sex standard for men and women."*

Mead's research was from before the emergence of Youth Culture in the 1950s. Perhaps of Western culture had been more like Samoa, there wouldn't have been as much of a need for Youth Culture in the first place.

Mead's research was criticised by **Derek Freeman (1983)** who lived in Samoa in the 1950s claimed Mead had exaggerated her picture of the guilt-free Samoan adolescence. He interviewed some of the Samoan girls and they denied their promiscuous behaviour, saying they had lied to Margaret Mead.

However, it is possible that contact with the outside world made the Samoans change their behaviour after Mead studied them (for example, they had converted to Christianity). Freeman was interviewing the Samoan girls now they were old women and perhaps felt embarrassed to admit their youthful behaviour.

Mead's research is an excellent starting point for any essay on Youth Culture. Her ***ethnomethodological approach*** *will feature in* ***2A; Research Methods.***

PERSPECTIVES ON YOUTH CULTURE

Perspectives are different ways of interpreting the social world. The four perspectives in this chapter are the ones introduced in **1A Socialisation, Culture & Identity** but another perspective (**Postmodernism**) is added and a sixth (**New Right**) will be introduced in **Chapter 3**.

Perspectives are very broad viewpoints. Individual sociologists from the same perspectives might disagree with each other. Some sociologists straddle more than one perspective. I will take a neutral view on which perspective is "right" or "wrong" and focus instead on how they differ and the ways in which they criticise each other.

CONSENSUS PERSPECTIVE: FUNCTIONALISM

Functionalism starts with the idea of a basic biological component to human social behaviour. This means that societies can be good or bad, based on how successfully that match our biological needs. Societies that go against our biological needs will be **dysfunctional** and throw up problems like unhappiness, crime and self-destructive behaviour.

Emile Durkheim, the founding figure of Functionalism, proposed that modern Capitalism was particularly difficult for people to make sense of, creating **anomie**, which is a state of disconnection from society that ultimately leads to suicide. Social institutions like the family have a function of reducing anomie by promoting **social integration** (a feeling of 'belonging').

Sharing a culture creates a **value consensus** – an agreed sense of how things should be done, what's important, the boundaries of acceptable behaviour and the things to be strived after.

Functionalists claim institutions have a **manifest** (obvious) **function** – something they do that benefits society. However, they also propose that institutions can have a **latent** (hidden) **function** – benefiting society in non-obvious ways.

Youth Culture is therefore a response to Capitalism and perhaps the weakening of institutions like religion. It promotes a sense of belonging (to a peer group) and gives young people a **set of values** to share. In particular, these values emphasise **freedom and transgression** (rules-breaking) to a greater degree than mainstream society. Functionalism buys into the '*Sturm und Drang*' view of Youth (p6) and identifies the **latent function** of allowing young people to 'let of steam' and vent frustrations in a safe way.

When Youth ends, young adults abandon Youth Culture as a 'phase' and adopt the values of mainstream culture. They look back on the transgressive things they did as youths with a mixture of embarrassment and nostalgia.

Of course, there are limits to transgression so Youth Culture cannot be allowed to get too out-of-hand. This is why **agencies of social control** are needed to establish the boundaries of what is acceptable even within Youth Culture.

Research: Go back over your notes on **1A Socialisation, Culture & Identity** and review **Peer Groups** and **Age Identity** as well as the ideas of **Durkheim (1912)**, **Parsons (1959)** and **Davis & Moore (1945)**, applying them to Youth Culture

CONFLICT PERSPECTIVE: MARXISM

Conflict is the opposite of consensus and **Marxists** reject the idea that society reflects human biological needs. Marxists believe that **society is shaped by conflict** between a **ruling class** that holds the wealth and power in society and a **working class** that is much more numerous but poor and powerless. For them, there are good and bad societies, with 'good' meaning 'giving power to the working classes' and 'bad' meaning 'allowing the ruling classes to hold all the power.'

For Marxists, Capitalism is not just complicated and stressful to live under, but outright unfair and oppressive. They reject the idea of value consensus because they think the rulers and the workers want very different things. **Ideology** is a set of beliefs that hides and justifies the unfairness in Capitalist society.

Youth Culture is therefore a response to Capitalism. However, while Functionalists see it as a sort of coping mechanism, Marxists see it either as **exploitation** or as **resistance**. Resistance falls short of being outright revolution, but it's still a refusal to join in the behaviour that Capitalism demands and a rejection of the **ruling class ideology** that justifies Capitalism.

Much of Youth Culture is exploitation: young people are being brainwashed into being obedient consumers and workers. They are being trained to value fashions and brands, to care about money and shopping, to value 'fitting in' and 'being popular' and to stigmatise genuine rebels as 'weirdos' and 'freaks.'

However, some **Youth Subcultures** (*c.f.* Chapter 2) actively resist Capitalism and show contempt for mainstream society and mainstream Youth Culture. Marxists see this response as much more authentic and valuable. These young people see the truth about society, if only for a short time.

Research: Go back over your notes on **1A Socialisation, Culture & Identity** and review **Peer Groups** and **Age Identity** as well as the ideas of **Bowles & Gintis (*Schooling In Capitalist America*, 1976)**, **Hebdige (1979)**, **Marx (1844)** and **Willis (*Learning To Labour*, 1977)**, applying them to Youth Culture

CONFLICT PERSPECTIVE: FEMINISM

Feminists argue that **gender** is a significant source of conflict in society. Feminists reject the idea that society's gender roles reflect human biological needs and argue that **society is structured in favour of the interests of males (patriarchy)**: although they make up half the population, women are subordinated to men, they are 'second class citizens' and are threatened with physical or sexual violence to keep them in line. Feminists reject the idea of value consensus because they think males and the females want very different things. They often make use of the Marxist concept of **ideology** – a set of beliefs that hides and justifies the patriarchy, persuading people to ignore or accept sexual discrimination as 'the way it has to be.'

Feminists take a similar view of Youth Culture, that it usually **exploits** young women but it can sometimes express **resistance** to patriarchy.

Youth Culture exploits young women by socialising them into accepting their subordinate roles: girls are encouraged to focus on personal beauty and popularity, acquiring boyfriends and accepting their status as **sex objects**. Girls who do not except this **heteronormative role** (i.e. a role that makes ordinary heterosexuality the rule) are **stigmatised**, often by teasing or bullying or rejection by peers.

However, some Youth Subcultures actively resist patriarchy, encouraging girls to support one another against sexism and encouraging **gender nonconformity**. Many Feminists see the increasing acceptance of nonbinary gender, lesbianism and transsexuality within Youth Culture as a positive thing rather than a cause for alarm.

Research: Go back over your notes on **1A Socialisation, Culture & Identity** and review **Peer Groups, Intersectional Identity** and **Age/Gender Identity** as well as the ideas of **Oakley (1982)**, **Faludi (*Stiffed*, 1999)** and **Crenshaw (*Mapping The Margins*, 1991)**, applying them to Youth Culture

SOCIAL ACTION PERSPECTIVE: INTERACTIONISM

The Consensus and Conflict Perspectives have something in common: they are **structuralist theories** and view society as a powerful set of institutions (the class system, the family, the workplace, religion, etc) that control human behaviour. There is very little possibility for **freewill**. Individuals are not very important in structuralist thinking.

The opposite is a **social action theory** that views individuals as having a lot of **agency** (the power to make changes). Social action theory views people as capable of resisting social control and altering the powerful institutions, when they choose to.

Structuralist theories are sometimes called **macro action theories** while social action is a **micro action theory** (macro meaning large, micro meaning small).

Symbolic Interactionism – or just **Interactionism**, for short – is a social action theory associated with **George Herbert Mead** and **Max Weber**. It views society as **the product of human interactions and the meanings that individuals give to those interactions**. It acknowledges that humans *create their own meanings*.

Youth Culture is partly something that shapes the way young people think and feel, but it's also the result of their thoughts and feelings. Young people can change Youth Culture. This goes against the idea that Youth Culture automatically exploits people or resists Capitalism. It *can* do those things, but it doesn't *have* to. It also goes against the idea that Youth Culture is just a phase young people go through: it *can* be that but it doesn't *have* to be.

Interactionists often use **Labelling Theory (Becker, *Outsiders*, 1963)** to explain how young people are labelled by society (e.g. as troublemakers, as irresponsible) and treated in accordance with those labels; if young people **internalise** those labels then a **Self-Fulfilling Prophecy (SFP)** can occur. Society can make stereotypes about young people come true through labelling. However, young people can negotiate those labels, redefining them. For example, society labels young people as 'lazy' but youngsters can respond by interpreting this as being 'cool' (not showing great concern or hurry over things) and viewing that as a positive thing.

Research: Go back over your notes on **1A Socialisation, Culture & Identity** and review **Intersectional Identity** and **Age Identity** as well as the ideas of **Becker** mentioned above, applying them to Youth Culture

POSTMODERN PERSPECTIVE: POSTMODERNISM

The Perspectives you have studied so far fit together in a sort of pattern. Functionalism (Consensus) is opposed by Marxism/Feminism (Conflict); all three are Structuralist views that are opposed by Interactionism (Social Action).

With Postmodernism, we have a completely different approach. It is sometimes called **'Post-Structuralism'** because instead of structures it emphasises **fragmentation** (things breaking apart) and **fluidity** (things changing into other things). Like Interactionism, it emphasises **choice** but it also draws attention to the **risk** and **uncertainty** that such choice involves.

Postmodernism is best understood as a set of linked ideas about society today:

After Modernity: We tend to use 'modern' to mean 'as things are now' but in Sociology it's a more specific term: a **modernity** is a society that develops science, industrialisation, national government, secularism (religion separated from public life) and individualism. You might think our society is *still like that*, but Postmodernists argue we have moved onto a new phase called **postmodernity** (meaning 'after modernity').

Young people in the 21st century have lived all their lives in postmodernity, creating a big generational divide with their parents who grew up in the 1980s or '90s (i.e. during modernity).

Media Saturation: The Mass Media, particularly the Internet, has invaded people's lives to a degree that the media shapes how people perceive the world. **Baudrillard (1970)** calls this chaotic, exciting but empty way of living **Hyper Reality**.

Young people in the 21st century are raised with access to tablets, digital TV channels and the Internet and experience Hyper Reality most strongly. **Faludi (*Stiffed*, 1999)** describes the Spur Posse, a gang of young men who were obsessed with being TV celebrities and who treated sexual assault like a TV game show.

Diversity, Choice & Fragmentation: Postmodern society is **multicultural** and affected by **Global Culture.** This means people living in postmodernity have an incredible **diversity** of **choices** available to them: religion (or lack of it), ethics, lifestyle, career, family, education; in fact, their **Identity**. This leads to **fragmentation** as the institutions that used to connect people break down, such as national governments losing authority, borders ceasing to matter, families becoming separated, beliefs becoming more individualistic.

These choices and the risk (see below) that goes with them press particularly on young people.

Fluidity, Risk & Uncertainty: In this fragmented society, choice becomes overwhelming. We no longer have any **certainty** about the right way to live, who to trust or what is true. Jobs tend not to be permanent, relationships are temporary: everything is **fluid**. This leads to a lot of anxiety, especially as all our choices come with great **risk**.

Fluidity means that the distinction between children and Youth is breaking down, as is the difference between Youth and adulthood. Instead, adults increasingly participate in Youth Culture as do children. This was recognised by **Postman (*The Disappearance of Childhood*, 1994)**.

'Death of Meta-Narratives': Part of this uncertainty is that the old explanations for things no longer satisfy people. These **'meta-narratives'** (or 'Big Stories') include religious teachings, political theories and **structuralist sociological Perspectives** like Marxism and Functionalism and even science itself. **Jean-Francois Lyotard (1979)** argues that the world has become too chaotic and changeable to be explicable by just one grand theory.

This means that Marxist ideas about **resisting Capitalism (Hebdige, 1979)** or Functionalist ideas about **Meritocracy (Davis & Moore, 1945)** are no longer credible explanations for Youth Culture.

Many sociologists accept there have been huge changes in society, but deny they amount to shift to Postmodernity. **Anthony Giddens (1999)** argues we are living in Late Modernity, the latest stage of modernity, characterised by extreme choice and risk, but still with much in common with previous generations.

Research: Go back over your notes on **1A Socialisation, Culture & Identity** and review **Global Culture, multiculturalism, Intersectional Identity** and the ideas of **Baudrillard, Davis & Moore, Faludi, Giddens, Hebdige** and **Postman** mentioned above, adding this Postmodern Perspective to them.

YOUTH CULTURE: A TOOLKIT

Youth Culture means the distinctive lifestyle of young people (teenagers). Youth Culture includes things like teenage food and drink, youth fashions and haircuts, teenage attitudes to politics or morality, pop music, video games, 'Young Adult' literature, movies & TV shows aimed at this audience, social media platforms preferred by young people and the sport they enjoy, as well as teenage etiquette, the drugs and sexual behaviour they think are acceptable.

AO2 ILLUSTRATION: YOUTH ONLINE

Whereas adults still watch the BBC or streaming services like Netflix, **YouTube** is the favourite for teenagers, with **Snapchat** and **Instagram** being more popular with teens than Facebook (preferred by their parents). New platforms like **TikTok** and **Twitch** are gaining popularity with young people. Young people are drawn to **vloggers** who post on these sites (also known as **'micro-influences'**) and there has been a rise in **social activism** online among young people, which has been nicknamed **'the Greta Effect'** after teenage environmental activist Greta Thunberg.

12-15 year olds
- 83% have their own smartphone
- 59% have their own tablet
- 81% use a smartphone to go online, **and** 69% use a tablet to go online
- 74% who own a mobile phone are allowed to take it to bed with them, while 61% of tablet owners are allowed to do this
- 36% use a smart speaker in the home
- 88% watch TV on a TV set, while 46% use a tablet, and 41% use a mobile phone to watch TV
- 98% watch TV programmes or films (on any device), for 11hrs 48mins a week
- 75% watch live broadcast TV, and 88% watch video-on-demand content*
- 81% play games, for 11hrs 36mins a week
- 72% play games online
- 89% watch YouTube, for 11hrs a week
- 41% watch YouTubers or vloggers
- 71% of online users have a social media profile

Source: Ofcom (2019)

Consensus vs Conflict

Functionalists see Youth as a necessary stage between childhood and adulthood. It is necessary because young people must be **integrated into society**. Children are socialised by their **family** and adults by the families they start and their **workplace** but young people are mostly socialised by their **peers**.

Talcott Parsons argues that, in a complex Capitalist society, young people need to be 'eased into' their adult roles. They take part-time jobs in preparation for careers, they date boyfriends or girlfriends in preparation for marriage, they loosen their ties to their parents in preparation for becoming fully independent: Youth is a period of preparation.

This is a **Consensus view** because it focuses on young people joining the wider community, learning its **norms and values** and figuring out how to fit in. It downplays the **deviant** behaviour of young people ("youthful high spirits!") and ignores the extent to which young people are **exploited** by employers and advertisers, **sexually predated upon** and the amount of depression and self-harm young people experience.

Marxists see Youth as an artificial category created by Capitalism. For example, the word "teenager" dates from the 1940s and was coined by American advertisers who had noticed the spending power of this age group and wanted to sell them comics, music, movies, cosmetics and (in America) cars.

Karl Marx argues that Capitalism creates **alienation** from your work and yourself and young people are experiencing this alienation for the first time and, in their different ways, try to **resist** it.

This is a **Conflict view** because it sees young people as the victims of a sort of Capitalist conspiracy to turn them into consumers – and then into obedient workers who need a wage to fund their consumption habits. Youth deviance and mental ill-health is a side-effect of this alienation. However, this view downplays the positive experiences that many young people have in part-time work and dating: the skills and responsibilities they learn at work, the emotional growth from teenage romance.

Feminists argue that young women are not just under pressure to accept their role as workers in the Capitalist economy, but a subordinate role too, oppressed by men. They learn to accept being sexually objectified (viewed as bodies for the sexual please of men), sexually harassed in the street and the workplace and subjected to sexual bullying by boyfriends. Much of this is catalogued in **Laura Bates' Everyday Sexism Project** (2012, https://everydaysexism.com/).

The **Sturm und Drang** ('Storm & Stress' p6) of Youth can be viewed from either angle. Consensus sees it as part of a difficult transition to adulthood and the emotional wrenching of breaking ties with parents and childhood security; Conflict sees it as a response to exploitation and the alienation of life in a Capitalist society that is only soothed by the brainwashing of **ruling class ideology**.

AO2 ILLUSTRATION: EVERYDAY SEXISM

Laura Bates worked as a nanny in her 20s but found the girls she looked after were strangely preoccupied with their body image and this was linked to the treatment they received in public and at school. She set up the **Everyday Sexism Project** in April 2012. She hoped to gather a hundred stories of sexual harassment in daily life, but her website quickly collected thousands and exceeded 100,000 testimonials in its first 3 years. Many of the stories were from young girls, including a 9-year-old who was sent a "dick pic" on her phone and many stories of being groped on public transport or verbally abused by passing strangers. Bates argues this behaviour is **normalised**: we accept it as normal, even though we shouldn't.

Bates herself received many death threats and rape threats. She writes in 2017: "*To be a feminist, I have learned, is to be accused of oversensitivity, hysteria and crying wolf. But in the face of the abuse the project uncovered, the sheer strength, ingenuity and humour of women shone like a beacon.*"

2012 is usually taken to be the beginning of the **4th Wave of Feminism**, which is focused on online activism and **Intersectionality**. Laura Bates' project is at the forefront of this. However, critics like **Germaine Greer (2014)** point out that much of the material on the Everyday Sexism website isn't sexist behaviour that has become normalised, but rather it is widespread criminal behaviour that isn't reported or punished.

AO2 ILLUSTRATION: THE ICE BUCKET CHALLENGE

This Challenge went viral on social media in the summer of 2014, started by US baseball player Peter Frates who was diagnosed with motor neurone disease (called ALS in America). The challenger tags a friend online, who must post up a video of themselves being doused with a bucket of icy water within 24 hours and challenge someone else. Typically, they must donate £100 to the medical charity, or just £10 if they perform the Challenge – although in some versions they pay nothing if they do the challenge and only pay if they decline it.

The Challenge raised £200 million worldwide and there were 2.4 million tagged videos on Facebook. Although celebrities and world leaders got involved, the Challenge was hugely popular among young people and spread by Youth Culture.

From a Consensus view, this shows shared moral values (giving to charity, supporting the sick) and introduces young people to charity activities. From a Conflict viewpoint, the Challenge is more of a stunt with the focus on narcissism (showing off) – the fact that many performers did the stunt *instead of* donating to charity makes it '**slacktivism**' (supporting a good cause with minimal commitment). It was also criticised for wasting water – 5 million gallons were used in 2014 at the same time as California was suffering a drought.

Online Youth Culture like this is a good example of a Postmodern Perspective: an obsession with media images is Hyper Reality becoming more important than real life.

RESEARCH PROFILE: EISENSTADT (1956)

Shmuel Eistenstadt (1923-2010) was a colleague of Talcott Parsons and his book *From Generation To Generation* (1956) develops Parsons' ideas further.

Eisenstadt accepts the Functionalist idea of *Sturm und Drang* ('storm & stress' in adolescence, p6) and links this to **anomie** brought on by isolation. Youth Culture and especially a peer group gives adolescents a vital sense of *belonging* (**social integration**).

Youth culture also allows adolescents to 'let off steam' in a safe way and **transgressive behaviour** (breaking the rules) by them is tolerated by society as part of 'youthful high spirits.' These transgressions are also important ways for young people to test the boundaries and experiment with norms and values. Ultimately, youthful transgressive behaviour contributes to social order by helping adolescents settle down as responsible adults.

A standard criticism of Parsons and Eisenstadt is that they were **middle class white males** writing in the 1950s. Their views only ever described a privileged section of society and, given the social changes since then (such as increasing **multiculturalism** and **Global Culture**), they might not apply to any section of society today.

However, Eisenstadt is not American but Israeli and Israel is a country with conscription of young people into the military at age 18. This might weaken Eisenstadt's arguments – or the similarity in his findings to the American Parsons might strengthen his claim to have identified universal functions of Youth Culture.

Research: other online youth trends and crazes (like Planking, Momo, Kylie Lips, Bottle Flipping, Blue Whale); youth protest movements or activism; trends/statistics for youth working & wages; visit the Everyday Sexism Project at https://everydaysexism.com/ and read the testimonies

Social Order & Control

Social Control is the way that society gets people to conform to mainstream norms and values. This is done through the **Agencies of Social Control** covered in **1A: Socialisation, Culture & Identity**. These agencies can be **formal** (like the police) or **informal** (like peer groups).

Young people are in many ways quite easy to control. They tend to live with their parents who monitor their behaviour. They are compelled to attend school. They do not have much money, depend on public transport and laws prevent them from doing many activities (like buying alcohol). Shops often only allow young people to enter in small groups and the police tell groups of youngsters to 'move along.' In addition, adults monitor young people informally and tend to report groups of youths 'loitering.'

Notice we have a special word for young people socialising in public places – 'loitering' implies they are up to no good. You never hear of elderly people being spotted 'loitering' in a park.

Young people find ways to avoid this social control. They often don't tell their parents where they are going and parents have trouble monitoring what their children are doing online. School is compulsory up to 18, but young people truant. Bicycles help young people get about and in Italy young people can travel on mopeds from age 14 – a striking part of Italian Youth Culture, especially as the requirement to get a licence was only introduced in 2004. Young people respond to monitoring with fashions that hide their identity, particularly hoodies.

A big **class difference** comes into effect, because middle class youths can meet and socialise at home: they have their own bedrooms and their parents have large houses where they can enjoy some privacy. They are more likely to have money to get into venues or travel and more likely to drive cars.

Working class youths often don't have homes that are large or private enough for this, or the money to go to other venues or drive cars. They are forced to socialise in public places, which means they draw attention and social control.

Feminists point out that young women are subjected to much more social control than males. This is largely informal, from family and peer groups: being labelled as a 'slag' is much more shaming for a girl than a boy. Parents monitor who their daughters befriend and date more closely than their sons. At the same time, sexually abusive behaviour from boys and young men is not challenged or punished (*c.f.* the **Everyone's Invited** website discussed in **1A Socialisation, Culture & Identity**).

AO2 ILLUSTRATION: NATIONAL SERVICE VS NCS

After World War II, young men aged 18-21 were required to serve in the military for 18 months. This was called 'National Service' and it lasted until 1960. These conscripts took part in military action in Malaya, Kenya and the Korean War. National Service acted as a **'rite of passage'** marking the end of Youth. For years afterwards, it was said of delinquent youths that "*some National Service would do 'em good!*" Recently **Prince Harry (2015)** has called for the reintroduction of National Service, saying: "*the army has done amazing things for me.*" Norway, Sweden and Israel are countries that still have compulsory military service for young men and women.

In 2011, the **National Citizenship Service (NCS)** was launched as a non-military (and non-compulsory) alternative to National Service. Groups of 16-17 year olds take a residential course, do physical and team building activities, learn life skills then plan and deliver a project to benefit the community. In 2018, more than 400,000 young people had taken part.

*I hope you can see the **Functionalist** thinking behind NCS and the idea that National Service would be 'good for young people.'*

Of course, **Marxists** are opposed to the idea of young people being conscripted into the Armed Forces and NCS is criticised for being too expensive for working class children and being a propaganda course for **ruling class ideology (Tania de St Croix, 2017)**.

RESEARCH PROFILE: CHAMBLISS (1973)

In 1973, **William Chambliss** published *The Saints & the Roughnecks*, an article describing two years spent observing Hannibal High School students (age 16-19) in America. He followed two gangs: six working class Roughnecks and eight middle class Saints. (The names of the gangs and the school are fictional to protect the anonymity of the boys and their families).

Chambliss observed that the Saints' behaviour was in many ways *worse* than the Roughnecks, engaging in truancy, under-age drinking, dangerous driving and vandalism. Yet they were seen as model students, whereas the Roughnecks were constantly in trouble with teachers and the police.

The Saints were successful in school, viewed as 'good students' by the teachers and found it easy to truant by pretending to have extracurricular activities. Since they had cars, they could travel to other suburbs or into the city to misbehave, where no one would recognise them. When they got into trouble with the police, they could pay fines and their parents would vouch for them.

The Roughnecks were viewed as delinquents. Their truancy was lower than the Saints, but it was public knowledge. Without cars, they had to gather in their own neighbourhood, where their fighting and drunkenness was observed. There were in trouble with the police and, while Chambliss observed them, each Roughneck was arrested at least once.

Chambliss uses **Labelling Theory** to explain his findings: the Saints had positive labels so their behaviour was interpreted as harmless; the Roughnecks were interpreted as delinquent because of their negative labels. The Saints went on to college and good jobs. The Roughnecks had different outcomes: attempted suicide, prison, gambling, unemployment.

Chambliss connects this to a **Marxist** understanding of class and privilege. Social control is imposed on the working classes, but not the middle classes, and this control *creates* deviancy rather than reducing it.

Chambliss' study is from the 1970s and the USA, so the results might not apply to 21st century schoolboys or the UK, where teenagers don't drive until they are 18 but they can legally buy alcohol before they are 21. The arrival of the Internet has changed the way young people socialise. The boys were white, so the study doesn't tell us about other ethnic groups or girls. The small sample size, although typical of **Interactionist** research, is hard to generalise from: these could have been unusual teenagers at an unusual school.

*Chambliss' study makes a great comparison for **Willis'** Learning To Labour (1973) where 'the Lads' behave similarly to Chambliss' Roughnecks (although they are a year or two younger). It is also interesting to compare with the Spur Posse observed by **Faludi** in Stiffed (1991).*

Research: respectable public figures with deviancy in their youth (e.g. Brett Kavanaugh in USA; David Cameron in UK); celebrities shamed by social media posts made in their teens; transgressive behaviour at elite private schools (e.g. www.everyonesinvited.uk/)

EXAM PRACTICE: YOUTH CULTURE

The OCR exam has three questions in **Paper 1 Section B**. Questions 4-6 are on Families & Relationships and questions 10-12 are on the Media, but this Study Guide is focused on Option 2, which contains questions 7-9:

7. Outline two explanations for the formation of youth culture. **[12 marks: 8 AO1 + 4 AO2]**

This is very similar to Q2 in Section A, but with no source A and B, so it has to come entirely from your own learning. Notice that the importance of AO1 and AO2 is switched: you get more marks for knowledge of Sociology here and far fewer for real life illustrations.

*Make two sociological points about youth culture – perhaps from a Consensus and a Conflict viewpoint. It's a good idea to refer to named sociologists (like Parsons, Eisenstadt, etc.) and you should definitely use some sociological terminology (like anomie, socialisation, social integration). Then offer examples of youth culture and make sure each example has an explanation of **why** it is youth culture. For example, "Pop music because many young people listen to the music, follow the musicians online and attend the gigs and festivals where they perform."*

8. Explain and briefly evaluate the view that youth culture is a form of social control. **[16 marks: 8 AO1 + 4 AO2 + 4 AO3]**

*This is similar to Q3 in Section A, but again with fewer marks given to AO2 illustration. The advice on writing 'brief evaluation' from **1A Socialisation, Culture & Identity** applies here.*

*Write three paragraphs. Each paragraph should introduce a sociological idea with some illustration from the real world. Each paragraph should finish off with a brief evaluation (see Chapter 5 for this). For example, you could write about the **Functionalist** idea of youth culture as preparation, then the **Marxist** idea of Capitalist exploitation, then finish off with **Eisenstadt's theory of testing boundaries and venting frustration** (p17).*

9. Assess feminist views about the role of youth culture. **[24 marks: 8 AO1 + 8 AO2 + 8 AO3]**

*This is a brand new style of question, with equal weight given to knowledge of Sociology, illustration and evaluation. The evaluation has to be developed evaluation; see **Chapter 6** for advice on this.*

*Write three paragraphs. Each paragraph should introduce a sociological idea with some illustration from the real world. Each paragraph should finish off with a developed evaluation (see Chapter 6 for this). For example, you could write about the idea of youth culture socialising girls into heteronormative roles, then the idea of youth culture helping young women to resist patriarchy, then finish off with **Laura Bates' Everyday Sexism Project** (p16) which exposes how widespread sexual harassment is.*

CHAPTER TWO – YOUTH SUBCULTURES

Subcultures were introduced in **1A: Socialisation, Culture & Identity** as a 'group within a group' that shares some of the **norms and values** of mainstream society but has norms and values of its own that might be seen as **deviant** (or at least unusual) by mainstream society.

In a way, Youth Culture is one gigantic subculture within society. When teenage Youth Culture was observed in the USA and UK in the 1950s, many commentators were disturbed by the appearance of this 'group within a group.' The phrase **'the Generation Gap'** was coined to refer to the difference between mainstream norms and values and the 'storm & stress' of teenage life, which seemed to be wild, irresponsible and sexually unrestrained.

Youth Subcultures quickly emerged within Youth Culture itself: the **Teddy Boys** of the 1950s (p43), the **Mods** (p29), **Rockers** and **Hippies** of the '70s and the **Skinheads** (p28) and **Punks** (p49) of the '70s. Later, **Goths** (p36), **Emos**, **Ravers** and other groups appeared, mostly linked to popular music. More recently, **Geek** (p26) subcultures linked to gaming, comics and computing have appeared.

Positive Views of Youth Subcultures

Youth Subcultures create an intense sense of belonging within a peer group. Because of the shared interest and often recognisable dress code, the subculture finds it easy to identify one another and integrate. Subcultures often draw in some of the most isolated or alienated young people who struggle to find a place within wider Youth Culture.

Subcultures can help young people with mental health problems, bullying, poverty or family abuse by offering supportive peers and a 'home away from home.' Some subcultures can also be involved in social activism, joining in protests and encouraging young people to question things mainstream society takes for granted.

Negative Views of Youth Subcultures

There's always a concern that Youth Culture separates young people from mainstream norms and values, but youth subcultures intensify this: they can be outright deviant. This can lead to young people being labelled as 'weirdos' and also bring them into contact with criminals (e.g. drug dealers) and trouble with the police.

Some youth subcultures reject Consumer Culture (e.g. **Punks**, p49) but others are strongly linked to it, meaning that youth subcultures can be a way for Capitalism to exploit young people by selling them products (music, fashion, the latest video games).

RESEARCH PROFILE: THE CENTRE FOR CONTEMPORARY CULTURAL STUDIES (CCCS, 1970s)

The **CCCS** was a research centre at the University of Birmingham, focused on **Neo-Marxist** Sociology – taking Marxist ideas about class conflict but using **Gramsci**'s idea about **Hegemony** rather than the traditional ruling class. It also used many techniques developed by **Interactionism** (p25) such as participant observation of small groups and **moral panics** (p57) in the Media.

It was founded in 1964 by **Stuart Hall** and continued working until 2002, but it is best known for its work on Youth Subcultures in the 1970s.

The CCCS publications included **Paul *Willis' Learning To Labour* (1977)** which studied 'the Lads' and **Dick Hebdige**'s *Subculture: The Meaning of Style* **(1979, p49)** which analysed Punks.

A major CCCS publication was the collection *Resistance Through Rituals* **(ed. Hall & Jefferson, 1976)**. This book proposed the idea that Youth Subcultures formed from working class youngsters resisting Capitalism and that much of the music, fashion and behaviour of youth subcultures needs to be interpreted as a rejection of Capitalist values and a commitment to **Working Class Identity**.

Contributors included **John Clarke** and **Phil Cohen** on Skinheads (p28), **Dick Hebdige** on Mods and **Tony Jefferson** (p44) on 1950s Teddy Boys.

A lot of this research involves **semiology**, which is a technique for interpreting **codes** (symbolic behaviour). For example, semiology is used to interpret Punk dress, language and music as resistance to Capitalism – but is it just delighting in shocking people? The problem with semiology is that the researcher's theoretical Perspective (i.e. Marxism) determines what how the researcher 'reads' the codes.

The CCCS researched at a time when the UK was rocked by conflict, with military attacks in Northern Ireland, mass unemployment, general strikes and later (in the 1980s) battles between police and strikers. These social circumstances might explain the youth subcultures that appeared, but they also might make the CCCS's ideas irrelevant now. However, supporters would argue these conflicts still exist in society, but in new forms (e.g. employment is now high, but many people work in the 'gig economy' for low wages and no security).

Research: find out about a youth subculture: Teddy Boys, Hippies, Mods, Rockers/Bikers, Skinheads, Punks, Goths, Emos, Ravers, Crusties – or a contemporary UK musical subculture like Drill, Grime or Makina; revisit your notes from **1A: Socialisation, Culture &* Identity** to place **Willis (1977)** in context

PERSPECTIVES ON YOUTH SUBCULTURES

Views on the importance and value of Youth Subcultures go to the heart of what makes the Perspectives different. They reveal a lot about views on **Consensus**, **Conflict** and **Social Order**.

CONSENSUS PERSPECTIVE: FUNCTIONALISM

Functionalism sees Youth Subcultures as part of the **transition** from family to workplace, which is a change from a loving and personal world where you are valued for who you are to a cold and impersonal one where you are valued for what you can do. Youth Culture in general helps with this transition, providing a sense of belonging to oppose **anomie**, but for some young people the transition is particularly difficult. These tend to be boys and the working class, because boys are more likely to move into full-time work (as opposed to motherhood) and working class people are more likely to work in dangerous impersonal conditions, like factories.

You can see the rather dated Functionalist ideas here: in the 21st century, working class people don't all work in factories and women don't automatically become housewives and mothers.

These pressures lead boys – especially working class boys – to create subcultures to ease the transition further. In a nutshell, because a bigger change is required of them, they have to make a bigger break with their childhood. Subcultures are a type of adaptation to difficult circumstances, like the cocoon a caterpillar enters to emerge as a butterfly.

Feminists criticise this view for the "*invisibility of women*" in it. **Marxists** argue that working class subcultures are about resisting Capitalism, not adapting to it.

This Functionalist view explains why most young people *don't* join subcultures and why older people *grow out of* their subcultures – but it fails to explain why particular subcultures take the forms they do (why do Skinheads shave their heads and wear workmen's boots? why do Punks wear torn clothes and spike their hair?).

Functionalism has an ambivalent (muddled, divided) attitude to subcultures. On the one hand, they are necessary phases in growing up for some people. On the other hand, they show a lot of **dysfunctional behaviour** and suggest a **failure of socialisation**, especially among the working class. Functionalism doesn't have a definite answer on whether Youth Subcultures are a **threat to social order** or a harmless (and ultimately beneficial) phase.

CONFLICT PERSPECTIVE: MARXISM

Marxism sees Youth Culture as a mixture of **exploitation** by and **resistance** to Capitalism. Youth Subcultures are seen as pure **resistance**. This is especially true of the subcultures studied by the CCCS in the 1960s and '70s, which were termed **Spectacular Youth Subcultures** because of their dramatic styles.

23

Middle class youngsters find it easy to 'play by the rules' in society because of their class position: they have **privileges** and don't encounter **oppression** or obstacles. Working class youngsters don't enjoy these privileges. Moreover, in the 1960s and '70s the industrial basis of working class life was changing: factories were closing and unemployment rising. Education claimed to be a **Meritocracy** for working class children but didn't offer **social mobility** for most of them. These young people perceive the Capitalist system to be a cheat and a lie and reject it; instead, they emphasise their **Working Class Identity**.

This analysis involves **semiology**: interpreting the codes of fashion and behaviour in symbolic ways. For example, wearing heavy denims and workingmen's boots is a code for **Working Class Identity**; wearing torn or homemade clothes is a code for rejecting **Consumer Culture**.

Feminists also complain about the "*invisibility of women*" in this Perspective. **Functionalists** point out that the conclusions of semiology reflect the researcher's starting point: if you start out *assuming* that subcultures are resisting Capitalism, you 'read' the codes to prove this. But this isn't really 'proof' and the codes could be 'read' in other ways.

Marxism also fails to explain why most young people **don't** join subcultures and why so many grow out of them in a few years. However, it does explain (through semiology) why the subcultures take the particular form they do.

CONFLICT PERSPECTIVE: FEMINISM

Feminists complain about the "*invisibility of women*" in studies of Youth Subculture. On the face of it, there **seem** to be more boys than girls in Spectacular Youth Subcultures, but this is for two reasons: (1) the researchers of the CCCS are **mostly male** and drawn to the more violent masculine behaviour in subcultures (**androcentric** or 'male-centred' **bias**), and (2) girls are **more socially controlled** by parents and teachers and attract **more negative labelling** for their deviant behaviour.

For example, there is a **double-standard** that makes it more acceptable for males to be outrageous or transgressive but females are condemned for doing this – even by the deviant males.

Feminists argue there is a **'bedroom culture'** for girls that exists in the privacy of the home. Girls can indulge in subcultural behaviour here (such as indulging in sexual fantasies about teen idols) while maintaining their reputation in public.

This analysis also involves **semiology**, which has similar problems to Marxism. It is much harder to gather **empirical** (fact-based) **evidence** about bedroom culture, because it isn't going on in public.

If social control of females weakens, you would expect female subcultures to move out of the bedroom and into the public sphere. This might explain the appearance of **'Ladettes'** in the 1990s (*c.f.* **1A: Socialisation, Culture & Identity**).

SOCIAL ACTION PERSPECTIVE: INTERACTIONISM

Interactionists reject the sort of structuralist explanations presented so far, like the idea that entire classes of people are behaving a certain way because of social forces. From an Interactionist viewpoint, Youth Subcultures *don't really exist*. Instead, there is a 'hard core' of innovative young people creating their own style (e.g. the 'true punks') and then a huge number of copycats who temporarily imitate aspects of that subculture, usually because the Media made it look interesting or glamorous.

This approach uses the idea of **societal reaction**. The Media picks on a few unconnected cases of young people producing unusual music or wearing exotic fashions. These cases really have nothing to do with each other, but the Media pulls them together in an **ideological framework** (an 'explanation that makes sense'), giving the phenomenon a title like 'punk.' All the people dressing like that or enjoying music like that are now labelled 'punks' even though they previously never saw themselves as a subculture.

A **Self-Fulfilling Prophecy (SFP)** takes place, as young people act out the labels and internalise them as a sense of **Identity**. Often, the Media fuels public outrage, which strengthens the sense of Identity. Eventually, the Media loses interest and, without it, the 'subculture' dissolves.

Interactionism is a good explanation of the Media's role in the formation of Youth Subcultures – see **Chapter 4** for a more detailed look at this. However, it is accused of being a *description* of subcultures forming rather than an *explanation*. For example, why does the Media single out certain individuals or groups in the first place? where does the ideological framework tying these behaviours together come from? why does the Media stir up outrage rather than, say, curiosity or admiration?

Marxists like **Stuart Hall (1978**, p40) claim to have the answer to this: the Media has a structural relationship to Capitalist institutions, so it regularly scapegoats young people to blame them for crises in Capitalism. The Interactionist account is incomplete without Marxism.

POSTMODERN PERSPECTIVE: POSTMODERNISM

Postmodernists agree with Interactionists that structuralist explanations of Youth Subcultures are implausible: they are **'Meta-Narratives'** that no longer make sense in a **fragmented** world. They also agree that the Media is involved, although they do not regard the Media as a **hegemonic** (leading, directing) force that provides a single ideological framework for things. In the 21st century, the Media is vast but fragmented, with people accessing different things online rather than reading the same things in newspapers.

Instead, Postmodernists argue we live in a **media-saturated society** and a **Hyper-Reality** where media images are more important than real events. We construct our identities from these media images, visiting what **Ted Polhemus (1997)** calls **'the Supermarket of Style.'**

This means that Youth Subcultures are becoming a thing of the past. Young people can pick and choose different style elements for their identity, like a collage: a bit of punk, a bit of geek, some hippie-chic. Polhemus argues that young people aren't willing to commit to one particular style and restrict their choices. Moreover, style is based on what people discover in the Media, rather than on their experiences in the real world away from Hyper Reality.

Michel Maffesoli (1996, p33**)** argues that subcultures have been replaced by more fluid **Neo-Tribes**.

As usual, Postmodernism is fascinating but imprecise. The Spectacular Youth Subcultures *do* seem to have faded but **Goths** (p36) are still with us and the **Geek Subculture** (p26) is flourishing. A generic sort of Youth Culture seems to have arisen, based around the Internet, night clubs, video games, etc. However, families and education still socialise people and Capitalism still exists: we don't live our entire lives online and we're not free to create any Identity we like, particularly if we are poor and working class.

AO2 ILLUSTRATION: GEEKS

The Geek Subculture is based around enthusiasm for obscure media (Japanese animation, video games, comic books, etc.) and includes activities such as role-playing games (e.g. *Dungeons and Dragons*), science fiction (e.g. *Star Trek*) and new technology.

Geek interests used to be marginalised in the 1970s and '80s but have become more mainstream. Comic book movie adaptations (e.g. *Marvel*) are now massive cinema hits. Science-fiction and fantasy-themed video games (e.g. *World of Warcraft*) have become multi-billion dollar industries and former-Geeks like **Steve Jobs** and **Bill Gates** have become influential billionaires. The first **San Diego Comic-Con** in 1970 drew 100 people; today the convention attracts 130,000 and major companies launch products there (like trailers for forthcoming movies). The TV sitcom **The Big Bang Theory** (2007-19) popularised Geek Subculture but also the stereotype of Geeks having poor social skills.

Mark Roeder (2014) argues that Geeks are in fact the next stage in human evolution: "*the high-tech environment … favours people with geek-like traits, many of whom are on the autism spectrum, ADHD, or dyslexia. Previously, such people may have been at a disadvantage, but now their unique cognitive traits enable some of them to resonate with the new technological zeitgeist and become very successful.*"

Unlike the **Spectacular Youth Subcultures** that fascinate Marxists (p48), the Geek Subculture is more middle-class and associated with academically-successful but socially-excluded young people. It's links to the Internet, imaginary worlds and role-playing link it to **Postmodernism**, as a subculture formed by **media-saturation** and **Hyper-Reality**.

Feminists complain that the Geek Subculture is often sexist and the term **'Geek Girl'** has become a insult among male Geeks, suggesting a woman who fakes an interest in Geek topics to gain attention.

YOUTH SUBCULTURES: A TOOLKIT

Youth Subcultures can be understood in relation to some of the aspects of **Identity** you learned about in **1A: Socialisation, Culture & Identity**.

YOUTH SUBCULTURES RELATED TO SOCIAL CLASS

This is the most common Identity related to subcultures. **Functionalists** and **Marxists** both see Class Identity as important for forming youth subcultures. For Functionalists, this is to help working class boys (in particular) adapt to their role in a Capitalist **Meritocracy**;

For Marxists, this is an insight into the **exploitative** nature of Capitalism, **resistance** to its values and a defiant statement of **Working Class Identity**.

Most Marxist research into this assumes that there is something misguided about Youth Subcultures: these young people are concerned about very real problems faced by working class communities that aren't being addressed by politicians or the mainstream media, but they express these concerns in unhelpful ways (e.g. through violence).

Functionalists are more inclined to explain the violence and deviancy through poor **Primary Socialisation** in the family (and poor **Secondary Socialisation** due to failing schools, the decline of religion and the rise of unemployment). For Functionalists, these subcultures aren't trying to make a muddled political statement, they're just behaving badly due to *Sturm und Drang* (p6).

Both Perspectives can be criticised for failing to address middle class Youth Subcultures, such as Hippies or Sloanes.

AO2 ILLUSTRATION: SKINHEADS

This Youth Subculture is famous for shaved heads, but also work boots (originally army surplus, later Doc Martens), jeans, braces and buttoned-down shirts. The 'uniform' represents working class pride.

There were two 'waves' of Skinhead subcultures. The first, in the 1960s, grew out of the Mod Subculture. These Skinheads (or 'Skins') listened to soul, ska and rocksteady (reggae) music – strongly influenced by the music of the Caribbean immigrants of the **Windrush Generation**. This mixing of White working class and Black Caribbean culture is a form of **Hybridity**.

A second wave of Skinhead Subcultures happened in the late 1970s, in response to Punk. These Skinheads listened to 2-Tone music (combining Ska and Punk) and were drawn into Far Right and White Supremacist politics – which is ironic, since Caribbean immigration influenced the first wave of Skinheads. However, there were anti-racist Skinheads who opposed these developments.

Research: listen to ska and rocksteady music like that of Desmond Dekker; find out about Hippies and/or Sloanes

RESEARCH PROFILE: CLARKE, COHEN (1976)

John Clarke and **Phil Cohen** were both sociologists from the CCCS and contributed to *Resistance Through Rituals* (1976). Both use **semiology** to explore how Skinhead Subcultures of the 1960s and early '70s express their norms and values through **codes**.

Clarke argues that Skinheads feel their working class community is under attack from Capitalism (through unemployment, changing work patterns, immigration, etc.) and respond by adopting an exaggeratedly working class and masculine appearance, based on the industrial and factory dress styles of their parents and grandparents.

Cohen argues that Skinheads is essentially territorial and based on the perception that working class areas are being lost because of Asian immigration. They oppose this symbolically through football hooliganism, which Cohen argues is meant to express ownership of the territory around the football ground. Cohen suggests that Skinhead violence is **symbolic resistance to social change** and an attempt to **'magically'** recreate a working class community. These are 'magical' because they offer young people a sense of strength and power but no practical solutions.

There's nothing very pretty about football hooliganism or racist violence. The tendency of Clarke and Cohen to reinterpret this as something noble or tragic (working class youths yearning for a lost community) should alert you to a problem with Neo-Marxist semiology: there's a risk of downplaying racism and hooliganism and portraying bad people as heroes.

YOUTH SUBCULTURES RELATED TO GENDER

Secondary Socialisation is the later influence of other people on your social experience. Children are influenced by their teachers, but also by youth leaders, religious leaders and later by employers. Peer groups (friends) and the media (TV, the Internet, pop music, video games) also affect our norms and values. The socialisation that continues into adulthood (for example, in the workplace) is sometimes termed Tertiary Socialisation (tertiary means "third").

AO2 ILLUSTRATION: MODS

This Youth Subculture is famous for close-cropped hair, smart shirts, thin ties and tailor-made suits. The 'unform' emphasises style and a good taste. Mods were associated with mopeds, especially stylish Italian scooters like Vespa.

They were also associated with using amphetamines (not illegal in the UK in the 1960s); the drug helped Mods stay up late socialising in coffee shops (British pubs all closed at 11pm but coffee shops often had live music). Early Mods listened to Modern Jazz and Blues, but later bands like The Who and Small Faces. The was a 'Mod Revival' in the 1970s led by The Jam.

Mods had an androgynous (mixing masculine and feminine features) look. Some male Mods wore lipstick and eyeshadow and there were prominent female Mods, who tended to wear men's trousers, flat shoes, very short hair and little makeup. Fashion designer **Mary Quant** invented the miniskirt and made Mod fashion mainstream. Women were drawn to the Mod Subculture because of the focus on style which made it easy to combine membership of the subculture with ordinary participation in work and school but also because it avoided the drunkenness and violence of other Youth Subcultures.

Research: listen to music popular with Mods: the Modern Jazz Quartet, The Kinks, The Who, Small Faces as well as the 1970s Mod revival music like The Jam

RESEARCH PROFILE: McROBBIE & GARBER (1976)

Angela McRobbie & Jenny Garber were published as part of *Resistance Through Rituals* (1976) but the criticised the CCCS for ignoring the role of women in favour of the male-dominated Spectacular Youth Subcultures. Male CCCS researchers tended to treat the girls as passive hangers-on.

McRobbie & Garber focus on one subculture where girls were quite prominent: the **Mod** Subculture. Mods placed importance on smart, fashionable clothing and the close-cropped hair created an androgynous (mixing masculine and feminine) look, making males and females appear similar. However, in the 1970s, girls experienced a **sexual double-standard** that meant even Mod males judged them harshly if the girls engaged in deviant behaviour.

Instead, the researchers focus on another female subculture called **Teenyboppers**. These teenage girls enjoyed pop music, focusing on 'teenage heart-throb' celebrities and girls' magazines (especially *Jackie*). The term 'bedroom culture' describes this private world where girls would meet at home, enjoy sleepovers ('pyjama parties') share magazines, experiment with fashion and makeup and gossip about boys. McRobbie & Garber argue that this is just as much **symbolic resistance to hegemonic Gender Identity** as the public behaviour of the boys; in the bedroom, the girls share taboo subjects (like sexual desire) and experiment with changing their appearance and Identity.

Critics argue that all girls are doing in the bedrooms is passively consuming media products like posters and magazines. McRobbie argues that this isn't so and girls are active consumers, resisting stereotypes and constructing their own **Gender**, **Class**, **Ethnic** and **Sexual** Identities.

YOUTH SUBCULTURES RELATED TO ETHNICITY

British Youth Culture has been influenced by immigrants, starting with the Windrush Generation. Both Mod and Skinhead culture developed out of Caribbean and Black American music. Ethnic minorities themselves are encouraged to **assimilate** and resemble the dominant White culture or engage in **cultural defence** and exaggerate features of the own culture.

Dick Hebdige (*Subculture: The Meaning of Style*, 1979) views Black Reggae and Rastafarian Subcultures as equally **resistance** to White culture and racism (p49).

Similarly, **Sanjiev Johal (*Brimful of Brasia*, 1998)** sees British Asians ('**Brasians**') as taking on a '**hyper-ethnic' style** to exaggerate their differences from the White community (by watching Bollywood cinema, listening to Bhangra music, etc.).

AO2 ILLUSTRATION: HIP-HOP

Hip-Hop grew out of Black American Culture in New York in the 1970s. The founders were **DJ Kool Herc** (who pioneered DJing with mixing decks and rapping), **Afrika Bambaataa** (who added break dancing and visual art with a spiritual philosophy) and **Grandmaster Flash** (who introduced scratching and other techniques for speeding and reversing the beats). This brought together the 4 Pillars of Hip-Hop Culture: (1) **DJing**, (2) **breaking dancing**, (3) **rapping**, and (4) **graffiti**.

The 'Golden Age of Hip-Hop' was the 1980s and '90s, when Rap music moved into the mainstream, distinguished by its use of sampling sound clips of movies and other songs. Copyright laws were brought in to restrict this style.

Hip-Hop fashion also became mainstream: baggy shirts, trainers and urban hairstyles. Street slang, later known as Ebonics, also crossed over: words like "*bling*" and "*diss*" have been added to the Oxford English Dictionary.

Women are prominent in Hip-Hop Culture but the arrival of 'Gangsta Rap' in the 1990s, with its themes of violence, drugs and masculine bagging, introduced **misogyny** (hostility to women).

Hip-Hop is now a part of **Global Culture** and, because it has been adopted by White fans (such as the rapper Eminem) and other ethnic groups, it is **Hybrid Culture** too.

Research: revisit your notes from **1A: Socialisation, Culture & Identity** and add details about **Back** and **Nayak** ('White Wannabes') and **Brah** (Asian code-switchers); listen to *The Message* (1982) by Grandmaster Flash & the Furious Five and *Rapper's Delight* (1979) by the Sugar Hill Gang to hear the early chart hits of Hip-Hop

RESEARCH PROFILE: CASHMORE (1997)

Ellis Cashmore (*The Black Culture Industry*, 1997) studied the origins of Hip-Hop, beginning in 1960s Jamaica. He traces it to the Bronx and other Black neighbourhoods of New York City in 1970s where mixing decks and a rapping Master of Ceremonies (MC) were features of outdoor block parties. By the 1980s, Rap music was promoted worldwide by big companies. However, Rap is constantly changing and as a result it has been adapted to suit a whole variety of Youth groups. Different cultures adopted Rap and added their own style to it.

Cashmore argues that this sort of **Hybridity** is a key characteristic of Hip-Hop, making it a truly **Postmodern** music genre and Subculture. However, Cashmore uses case studies of the Motown record label and the careers of Michael Jackson and Prince to argue that Black music has been turned into a **commodity** (a product to be sold) for White-controlled corporations, losing its authenticity and its ability to challenge racial injustice.

More recent critics have complained that commercial Rap music contributes to negative stereotypes of Black youths as criminals, Black women as sex objects and normalising sexism, violence and drug use. Others argue that Rap music is empowering for Black youths facing racism and poverty.

YOUTH SUBCULTURES RELATED TO HYBRIDITY

We have already seen that most Youth Subcultures are **Hybrid Cultures**: Mods and Skinheads both drew on Caribbean musical and fashion influences and White youngsters have embraced Hip-Hop. **Dick Hebdige (1979**, p49**)** claims that **Spectacular Youth Subcultures** can be read **semiologically** as *"responses to the black immigrant presence in Britain."*

Postmodernists argue this hybridity has gone even further with the arrival, since the 1990s, of **Global Culture** and the Internet. Youth Culture in general is now about 'picking and mixing' stylistic elements from other cultures as well as a 'retro' element of nostalgia. A lot of young people listen to playlists (e.g. on services like Spotify) where pop music from the 1960s sits next to the latest R&B.

Paul Willis (1990) argues that the Spectacular Youth Subcultures are fading because there are so many **'style and taste cultures'** available for young people to define their Identity. **Willis (1990)** argues that young people engage in **symbolic creativity** in the way they adopt fashion and leisure products to create their own unique style. This is similar to **Polhemus'** **'Supermarket of Style**.'

Critics argue that there are *still* Youth Subcultures (e.g. Goths, p36).

Hollands & Chatterton (2002) complain that mainstream Youth Culture is increasingly dominated by **Consumer Culture**, where young people visit corporately owned bars and nightclubs, listen to commercial chart music and dress in high street fashions in a **passive** rather than a creative way. However, there are still 'alternative' and 'authentic' subcultural venues outside the mainstream for young people who go outside the centres of towns and cities (an example would be Makina, *below*).

AO2 ILLUSTRATION: MAKINA

Makina is Spanish hardcore techno music with rapid rap-style MCing that has become 'the sound of the North East of England.' It emerged from clubs like the New Monkey in Sunderland in the 1990s. These venues didn't serve alcohol so young people were allowed in at 16 – although the New Monkey was closed down in 2006 for drug offences there. Makina might be of Spanish origin, but it is rooted in the experiences of the poorest estates in Newcastle, Sunderland and Middlesbrough, with lyrics about partying, stealing cars, being chased by the police and doing drugs, but not the consumerist bragging about fashion labels and the misogyny about women found in Gangsta Rap.

Music journalist **Joe Muggs (2014)** calls Makina *"proper, in-the-foundations-of-the-city, cross-generational folk music"* which means it has an authenticity that commercial pop and R&B don't have as well as being part of the Youth Culture of the North East.

Mark Rimmer (2010) carried out an ethnographic study of Makina fans from a deprived Newcastle housing estate and concludes the music helps them *"help them think through the somewhat contradictory processes at work"* in their community.

Research: listen to Makina music or better still watch ***Makina!* (dir. Aponysus, 2020)**, a 20 minute British Council documentary about the music and the subculture; revisit your notes from **1A: Socialisation, Culture & Identity** and apply **Thornton**'s ideas of **subcultural capital** to this.

RESEARCH PROFILE: MAFFESOLI (1977)

It's an important insight of Postmodernism that Identities like Class become unstable in a fluid postmodern culture. French sociologist **Michel Maffesoli (*The Time of the Tribes*, 1996)** argues that Youth Culture and Subcultures have been replaced by 'urban tribes' or **Neo-Tribes**.

Maffesoli's ideas are explored by **Andy Bennet (*Subcultures or Neo-Tribes?*, 1999)** who studied the Newcastle nightclub scene in the 1990s (including **Makina**, *above*). He found young people didn't define themselves as members of any particular group, mixed and matched musical tastes and shared interests and lifestyle in common rather than social class or values.

Bennet discovered these Neo-Tribes are much more **fluid** than the old Youth Subcultures: a young person could belong to several and drift from one to another. An analogy would be a multi-dancefloor nightclub where young people could go from venues playing Rap to commercial pop to hard rock or retro music, mingling with different people in each environment.

EXAM PRACTICE: YOUTH SUBCULTURES

The OCR exam has three questions in **Paper 1 Section B**. Questions 4-6 are on Families & Relationships and questions 10-12 are on the Media, but this Study Guide is focused on Option 2, which contains questions 7-9:

7. Outline two ways youth subcultures are related to ethnicity. **[12 marks: 8 AO1 + 4 AO2]**

This is very similar to Q2 in Section A, but with no source A and B; you get more marks for knowledge of Sociology here and far fewer for real life illustrations.

*Make two sociological points about ethnic subcultures – perhaps from a Consensus/assimilation and a Conflict/cultural defence viewpoint. It's a good idea to refer to named sociologists (like Johal) and you should definitely use some sociological terminology (like Brasians, hyper-ethnicity, code-switching). Then offer examples of subculture and make sure each example has an explanation of **why** it is an ethnic subculture. For example, "Hi-hop because it came out of the experiences of poor Black Americans living in New York in the 1970s."*

8. Explain and briefly evaluate the view that youth subcultures are related to hybridity. **[16 marks: 8 AO1 + 4 AO2 + 4 AO3]**

This is similar to Q3 in Section A, but with fewer marks given to AO2 illustration.

*Write three paragraphs. Each paragraph should introduce a sociological idea with some illustration from the real world. Each paragraph should finish off with a brief evaluation. For example, you could write about the **Postmodernist** idea of fluidity using Makina as an example, then the argument for the disappearance of Spectacular Youth Subcultures, then finish off with **Maffesoli's theory of Neo-Tribes** (p33).*

9. Assess the view that youth subcultures are a form of resistance to Capitalism. **[24 marks: 8 AO1 + 8 AO2 + 8 AO3]**

*This is a question with equal weight given to knowledge of Sociology, illustration and evaluation. The evaluation has to be developed evaluation; see **Chapter 6** for advice on this.*

Write three paragraphs. Each paragraph should introduce a sociological idea with some illustration from the real world. Each paragraph should finish off with a developed evaluation. For example, you could write about the idea of Spectacular Youth Subcultures like Skinheads resisting Capitalism, then consider Mods or Punks, then finish off with the argument that these Spectacular Youth Subcultures have faded and been replaced by passive consumers.

CHAPTER THREE – DEVIANT SUBCULTURES

Deviance is going against the **norms** and/or **values** of society. A similar term is **transgression**, which means more specifically going against the rules or laws.

There has been concern about Youth Deviance since Youth Culture first emerged in the 1950s and the idea that Youth was a period of irrational **'Storm & Stress'** goes back even further (**Hall, 1904**). Some Youth Subcultures seem to take a delight in being transgressive, with shocking fashions, offensive language and celebrating anti-social behaviour.

Positive Views of Youth Deviance

Even if young people are deviant, that might not be a bad thing. Society *needs* a certain level of deviance so that there can be progress and innovation. Young people have to break the rules to come up with new ideas. **Mary Quant**'s miniskirt was shocking when it first appeared in 1963. Over time, if society reacts positively to this deviance, it moves into the mainstream, as can be seen with **Hip-Hop**. This view is associated with **Functionalism**.

A different view is that youth deviance is a justified response to real problems in society. Young people have not yet settled into social roles, they still have ideals and social norms that adults take for granted are seen by the young with fresh eyes. Young people reject society and express this rejection by breaking the rules. Their deviance is an act of **resistance** through symbolic **rituals**, albeit an ultimately ineffective one.

This view is associated with **Conflict Perspectives**, especially **Neo-Marxism**.

Negative Views of Youth Deviance

Even if a small amount of youth deviance benefits society, a lot of it can poison society. Youth Deviance can be self-harming (such as taking drugs and truanting school) and it harms the community (such as vandalising public buildings or intimidating neighbours and shoppers). When youth deviance tips into violence, it can take the form of gang warfare or racist hate, which terrifies and oppresses innocent people. This sort of extreme deviance is a symptom that something is wrong on a deeper level in society.

This view is associated with **Functionalism** and especially the **New Right Perspective** (p38). It used to be rejected by **Marxism**, which interpreted youth deviance in a rather heroic light or else regarded it as **scaremongering and scapegoating** of young people from working class backgrounds. However, **Neo-Marxists** (p40) recognise that not all youth deviance targets Capitalism: other poor people and ethnic minorities are often the victims.

AO2 ILLUSTRATION: GOTHS

Goths are a Youth Subculture that grew out of Punk in the early 1980s. Goths dress in black, often in fashions linked to sexual fetishes (leather, bondage) or 19th century glamour (lace, corsets). White face makeup is popular, with dramatic eye makeup and dyed black hair, often outrageously styled. Body piercing is popular. The overall appearance is related to horror genres, such as vampires and zombies. The subculture embraces melancholy and the dark aspect of life.

Gothic music was pioneered by **Siouxsie & the Banshees** (Siouxsie Sioux established the Gothic look), **Joy Division** and **The Cure**. The music tends to be gloomy with lyrics that explore alienation, mental ill health and suicide as well as horror themes.

Paul Hodkinson (2002) argues that Goths remain a Spectacular Youth Subculture, contrary to theories that these subcultures have declined, and argues that, unlike Punk, members remain part of the subculture long into adulthood.

In 2007, **Sophie Lancaster** and her boyfriend Robert Maltby were attacked in a park by a gang of teenagers because of their Goth appearance. Sophie was murdered. There was a petition to widen the definition of Hate Crime to include attacks on subcultures like Goths.

Goths are a subculture with strongly deviant appearances and interests, but who are not violent or associated with conflict. Membership of the subculture is more like to make you a *victim* or violence than a perpetrator.

Research: listen to Goth music; find out more about the murder of Sophie Lancaster.

Goth couple (photo: fluffy_steve)

RESEARCH PROFILE: DURKHEIM (1895)

Emile Durkheim, a Functionalist and founder of Sociology, wrote *The Rules of Sociological Method* (1895) in which he describes the 'society of saints' where everyone is an "*exemplary individual*" and "*crimes are unknown.*" Durkheim argues that there will still be "*faults*" among the saints. These faults appear trivial to outsiders but among the saints they cause "*the same scandal that the ordinary offense does in ordinary consciousness.*"

Durkheim's insight is that deviance is **relative**. In a society where everyone is well-behaved, then sneezing in public or a mild swear word will bring fierce sanctions. In a society of barbarians or outlaws, no one bothers with sneezing or swearing, but murder or cannibalism will bring the same fierce sanctions. There will always be deviance because there will always be rules that can be broken and how trivial or serious the transgression is depends on how well-behaved everyone else is.

PERSPECTIVES ON YOUTH DEVIANCE

Perspectives are very broad viewpoints but they tend to fall into the camps outlined above, either seeing youth deviance as necessary/admirable or as a danger.

CONSENSUS PERSPECTIVE: FUNCTIONALISM

Functionalists believe in the importance of value consensus in society, which is reinforced is through **policing the margins**: agencies of social control reward those who conform or punish those who deviate. Shared disapproval of deviance actually strengthens social solidarity.

Kingsley Davies (1967) suggests deviance acts as a safety valve for society. By engaging in deviance, people 'et off steam' and can return to their respectable lives.

Davies gives the example of prostitution, suggesting that visiting prostitutes makes it easier for men to stay married. This argument isn't just weird and out-of-date: it shows a problem with Functionalism, that it is prepared to make excuses for social evils if they are somehow 'in the common good.'

The isolation people experience in Capitalist societies increased deviance. Rapid change increased deviance because of anomie: the collapse of social control and social solidity. Young people are particularly isolated, so their subcultures are more likely to be deviant.

Many people criticise the idea that deviance is normal and functional. Crime is a serious problem for victims and for society and we should be trying to prevent crime, not excuse it. **Feminists** object to the idea that the exploitation or abuse of women is made acceptable if it helps society function.

Marxists argue that laws are made by the state and work in the interests of the ruling class. Instead of value consensus, they argue there is **ideology** or **hegemony** supporting capitalism.

Traditional Functionalism does not consider why some people commit crime and others do not. Most people do not commit crime.

The New Right

The New Right could be considered a 'spin-off' from Functionalism in the 1980s. Its central assumption is that the vital value consensus has either collapsed or is about to collapse, so emergency measures are needed to restore it.

The New Right diagnoses the core institution for value consensus as the nuclear family (married parents and their children) and the biggest threat to this as the **Welfare State**. The Welfare State is the political arrangement that pays benefits to the poor and the unemployed.

Critics of the Welfare State argue it **rewards worklessness** and **undermines the family** (since couples are not forced to stay together for monetary reasons if the state pays for their children).The single parent family (especially the single mother with children) is a focus for the New Right, who argue that single parents cannot effectively **socialise** their children, who grow up 'feral': the girls get pregnant without marrying and live on child benefits, repeating the cycle' the boys search for a father-figure and join **gangs**.

The New Right identifies a **'benefits trap'** that means unemployed people would end up worse off if they took a job, creating an incentive to stay unemployed and leading **to generational unemployment**, where families have parents and grandparents who do not work and claim benefits. The solution is to cut back benefits, forcing health adults to find work and take responsibility for their families.

*These are controversial arguments. Many people (including but not limited to **Marxists**) would argue that unemployed people desperately want to work. The decline of British industry in the 1970s and '80s mean that there isn't work to find in some deprived communities and the rise of the 'gig economy' means such work as can be found won't support a family.*

One of the main speakers for the New Right is American sociologist **Charles Murray (1984)**, who warns that the benefits trap and the collapse of the nuclear family has created an '**underclass.**' The underclass is made up of single parent families on benefits, where the mothers cannot control their children and fathers avoid their responsibilities, living a life of petty crime.

Research: revisit your notes on **1A; Socialisation, Culture & Identity** and link these ideas to **Charles Murray** and **social control in the workforce** – including the arguments by the **Joseph Rowntree Foundation (2012)** and **Macmillan (2011)** that cast doubt on the existence of Murray's underclass.

Culture & Identity

Functionalism has produced another spin-off called **Subcultural Theory** to explain deviant subcultures. Some focus on how some young people experience frustration in their attempts to be successful at school and respond by forming an **Anti-School Subculture** (p48).

A different approach comes from **Walter B Miller (1958)** who argues that 'lower class' people already exist in a subculture which has distinctive values that are different from the mainstream. He calls these subcultural values **'Focal Concerns'** and they include thinks like **Excitement** (needing short term thrills) and **Toughness** (needing to prove your strength to others). An interesting Focal Concern is **Fatalism**: believing nothing you can do will change what's going to happen so there's no point in trying. Middle class children are supposedly raised with the belief that they can decide their own future, which is why they embrace **Meritocracy**.

These Focal Concerns don't automatically make a working class youth deviant, but they make it more likely, especially when they are strongly **internalised** through **socialisation** to form a **Deviant Identity**.

Miller's ideas are rather vague: just who exactly are the 'lower classes' and how do you measure Focal Concerns? Some would say Miller is just recycling snobby prejudices about the poor.

This Subcultural Theory is criticised for ignoring girls and applying mainly to White boys. More importantly, it seems to give up a very important principle of Functionalism, which is that there is **value consensus** in society. It implies that the working classes are a separate culture in conflict with middle class culture and this is an idea that you normally find in **Marxism**.

CONFLICT PERSPECTIVE: MARXISM

Marxists don't accept that deviance comes from being badly socialised and they certainly don't agree that there's something inherently deviant about being working class.

Instead, Marxists argue that Capitalism itself is **criminogenic** – it is a system that creates crime and drives people to commit crime. **Young (1984)** claims we live in a 'bulimic society' where the constant need to get the latest products, brands and fashions causes people to become deranged.

For Marxists, the real criminals are the rulers of the Capitalist system and they argue that the **White Collar Crime** carried out by corporations does far more damage to society than muggers or hooligans on the streets.

However, **ruling class ideology** (especially as it is presented through the **Media**) causes people to focus on the wrong things. People have an exaggerated fear of street crime and working class youths, but dismiss white collar crime as harmless or unimportant. The police crack down on working class youths, but don't pursue white collar criminals; this is called **selective enforcement**.

This can be explained by **Althusser (1970)** who identifies the **Ideological State Apparatus** (ISA, e.g. the Media) and the **Repressive State Apparatus** (**RSA**, e.g. the police) which combine to support Capitalism.

Research: revisit your notes on **1A: Socialisation, Culture & Identity** and link these ideas to **Jock Young**, **Edwin Sutherland** and **Louis Althusser**.

Neo-Marxism

Neo means 'new' and Neo-Marxism emerged in the 1970s as update of Marxist thought. A big inspiration was **Antonio Gramsci (1891-1937)** who moved away from the idea of a revolution to overthrow Capitalism. Gramsci observed that the ruling class was no longer a literal class of aristocrats and factory owners, but had become a **Hegemony**, a confederation of influential people with a vested interest in keeping Capitalism going. Gramsci pointed out that Hegemony **'manufactures consent'** through education and the Media.

The **CCCS** (p22) developed Neo-Marxism in books like *Resistance Through Rituals* **(1975)**. Youth Subcultures are only 'deviant' in hegemonic terms – they are presented that way by the Media in order to make them seem like the real enemy. In fact, working class youths are engaged in a **counter-hegemonic struggle**. Since they cannot literally tear down Capitalism, they do so symbolically, through '**rituals**' like **Punk** music (p49) or **Skinhead** fashions (p28).

A key member of the CCCS is **Stuart Hall** who wrote *Policing The Crisis* **(1978)** at a time when the UK was rocked by strikes and suffering mass unemployment. Hall points out that the British newspapers started a **moral panic** (p57) about **Black muggers** at a time when there was a genuine chance of Capitalism collapsing. This distracted people from the crisis, inflamed hostility between the White and Black working classes and justified police crackdowns.

This is termed the **'divide & rule'** approach to Hegemonic control: make the non-hegemonic groups (the White and Black working classes) hostile to each other so they never unite to challenge hegemonic power. The White working class welcome the deployment of heavy policing, because they believe (wrongly) it is protecting them. Hall claims this is **manufacture of consent** in action.

Hall (and notice this Hall is not the same as G Stanley Hall who coined 'Storm & Stress') wrote an absolute classic with **Policing The Crisis** *but has been attacked for creating a* **conspiracy theory** *since it's not clear exactly how the newspapers united in this way. Moreover, negative stereotypes against the Black working classes existed before and continued after the 'Crisis.'*

Neo-Marxism has been influential in Left Wing politics. It paints a more complex picture than the hard-done-by Proletariat rising up against the wealthy Bourgeoisie who want to keep them down-trodden. Instead, there is a struggle going on at every level of society between different groups and ideas and this struggle is often symbolic. This insight leads to **Intersectionalism**, which focuses on a plurality of privileged and oppressed identities and views language itself as a force for oppression.

Culture & Identity

The work of the CCCS is sometimes termed '**Marxist Subcultural Theory**.'

It assumes that most adults find it hard to resist **hegemonic control** because they are trapped by family responsibilities and careers. Young people are not yet trapped: they don't have family responsibilities, they might only work part-time or be unemployed. They are more able to resist hegemony.

Each generation of working class youth faces similar problems but in different social and cultural circumstances. Each group adopts a style (dress, speech, music, behaviour) based on their circumstances and expresses their **resistance** through this style. **Mods** reflect the circumstances of the 1960s by displaying their wealth through sharp suits and Mary Quant fashions; **Punks** reflect the 1970s by displaying their contempt for conventional values. The Punk band the Sex Pistols famously used the F-word on live TV in 1976, triggering mass complaints.

Mike Brake (1980) calls these 'magical solutions' because they do not really change the way society is structured. But they are meaningful to the members of the subculture as part of their Identity.

Marxist Subcultural Theory is challenged by pointing out in only focuses on resistance and it ignores subcultures like **Geeks** (p26) who are quite conservative and embrace **Consumer Culture** (although often an obscure part of it). Similarly, it doesn't pay enough attention to how Youth Subcultures are manipulated by advertisers and businesses.

Finally, it can be accused of glamorising Youth Subcultures as heroic underdogs, when some of these youths are violent and racist criminals.

SOCIAL ACTION PERSPECTIVE: INTERACTIONISM

The Interactionist Perspective sees young people as negotiating their Identity through a series of interactions with their peers, their parents and the state.

David Matza (1964) suggests **Drift Theory**. He argues that there aren't really any deviant Youth Subcultures. All groups in society share **subterranean values**: deviant urges to go against social norms, such as partying hard, drinking, swearing, fighting or having sex with the wrong people. We keep these urges under control and act on **conventional values**, but indulge these urges at leisure times (weekends, holidays abroad). We 'drift' between conforming and deviant behaviour. **Restraining your subterranean values** and **indulge them safely** is a learned skill, so young people are more likely to do it inappropriately, at the wrong time, in the wrong place.

Culture & Identity

Edwin Lemert (1967) points out a distinction between **primary and secondary deviance**.

Primary deviance is something everybody does: we've all stolen things (if only pens from the office or towels from the hotel), broken the law, damaged things that don't belonged to us, had romantic interactions with someone we shouldn't, used obscene language or been violent. Most of the time it goes unnoticed and there are no consequences.

Secondary deviance is deviance that society reacts to. Someone 'calls it out' and assigns a label: we are blamed, accused; people are shocked; the authorities step in. This includes being labelled as a criminal (or a 'thug' or a 'punk' or a 'slut'). At first this label doesn't conform to our self-image and that leads to anxiety. Eventually, we alter our self-image to conform to the label: this is the **Self-Fulfilling Prophecy (SFP)**.

Some labels have **Master Status** and are particularly hard to negotiate or remove. If you are labelled as 'lazy' you can negotiate that label (*'I'm only lazy with subjects I don't enjoy'*) or prove it wrong. If you are labelled as a criminal. It's hard to negotiate (it's no good saying you're not a criminal because you only steal from rich people) or remove – the label can stick for years.

Entire Subcultures can be labelled as 'deviant' as a group. If you imitate Punk fashions, you acquire secondary deviance, a deviant label that you cannot negotiate and you end up becoming the violent thug society expects you to be.

Since young people have less power in society, it's harder for them to avoid secondary deviance or negotiate deviant labels. This is why they get deviant labels more than adults.

Critics say that secondary deviance is only a good explanation of delinquency and non-serious crime; it's hard to argue that murder is only regarded as criminal because society labels it that way. It's also hard to see how labelling can explain hidden crimes like child abuse.

Research: revisit your notes on **1A: Socialisation, Culture & Identity** and link these ideas to **Howard Becker**

YOUTH DEVIANCE: A TOOLKIT

You need to know about four specific types of deviant Youth Subcultures and some of the statistical trends about youth deviance in UK society.

DELINQUENT SUBCULTURES

Delinquency is a term for youth deviance: the sort of antisocial behaviour that teenagers get up to which falls short of being criminal or counts as **petty crime** (non-serious crime). Examples include truanting, under-age drinking and smoking, swearing, fighting, shoplifting and joyriding (stealing a car, driving it for fun then abandoning it).

Matza's Drift Theory (p42) and **Miller's Focal Concerns** (p39) are good explanations (up to a point) of delinquent subcultures. Most youths grow out of delinquent behaviour, although Matza points out that adults carry on expressing subterranean values, but less publicly. **Chambliss' study of the Saints & the Roughnecks** (p19) is a good account of delinquency linked to **labelling**.

AO2 ILLUSTRATION: TEDDY BOYS

Teddy Boys – or Teds – were Britain's first Youth Subculture from the 1950s. They came to public attention after the film *Rock Around the Clock* (1956) arrived in British cinemas: young Teds rioted in the cinemas, slashing seats and throwing bottles, then fought with the police in the street. The newspapers started a **moral panic** (p57) about the 'teen menace.'

Teddy Boys were also involved in the **1958 Notting Hill Race Riots**.

Teddy Boys wore velvet jackets, suede shoes (known as brothel-creepers or beetle-crushers) and bootlace ties. They greased their hair and styled it with fringes called quiffs. The clothing was based on Edwardian fashion (1901-1910) mixed with American influences (like the ties) because of their love of American rock'n'roll.

They also listened to Black American music like jazz and blues; similar to **Skinheads** (p28), they loved Black music but were hostile to Black immigrants who were arriving in Britain as part of the **Windrush Generation**.

Teddy Girls (also called Judies) wore the same long jackets, pencil skirts or rolled-up jeans and hair in ponytails. The glamorous look was a rejection of post-War 'Austerity' – in the UK at this time, clothing was expensive and fashions were monotonous and drab for ordinary people.

Research: *Rock Around the Clock*; more about Teddy Boys & Girls; Windrush Generation; Notting Hill riots; post-War Austerity

CRIMINAL SUBCULTURES

A criminal subculture is more organised than a delinquent one; delinquents might commit petty crime but criminal subcultures are focused on crime like drug-dealing, theft or extortion (taking money by threats).

AO2 ILLUSTRATION: YARDIES & RUDEBOYS

The first Caribbean immigrants to the UK in the 1950s were sometimes nicknamed 'yardies' and they contributed a lot to British culture, especially in music, but were moistly working-age adults looking for jobs. Back in Jamaica, in poverty-stricken Trenchtown, violent street gangs emerged in the 1970s, known as Yardies or Posses.

A government crackdown in the '80s meant some of these Yardies migrated to the UK. Yardies have been linked to gun crime and dealing in marijuana and crack cocaine.

Some critics suggest Yardies are a Media-driven **moral panic** (p57) and not a real criminal subculture at all.

Yardies are not a Spectacular Youth Subculture (p48) but have some links to the Caribbean Rudeboy Subculture of the 1960s. Rudeboys listened to ska and rocksteady music – and later reggae – and wore sharp suits and pork pie or trilby hats. They influenced the tastes of **Mods** (p29) and **Skinheads** (p28). 'Rudeboy' has become a part of 21st century urban slang and a greeting.

Research: Yardies and the 1993 murder of PC Patrick Dunne; Rudeboys; listen to rocksteady, ska and reggae music

RESEARCH PROFILE: CLOWARD & OHLIN (1960)

Cloward & Ohlin are Functionalists who argue that, alongside the **legitimate opportunity structure** (school, jobs, careers – the **Meritocracy**) there is an **illegitimate opportunity structure** (a career in crime). Just as not all people can access the legitimate opportunity structure (because of poor qualifications, unemployment, etc.), the illegitimate opportunity structures aren't available to everyone either.

Cloward & Ohlin identify three illegitimate opportunity structures: **(1) Criminal**, which is organised, like the Mafia, with a 'career path' for young recruits that mirrors the legitimate meritocratic structures (bonuses for good work, promotions, etc.); **(2) Conflict**, where gangs compete over territory ("turf wars"), which is violent and only occasional lucrative (some money from drugs or theft); **(3) Retreatist**, where groups who cannot join organised crime or gangs simply 'drop out' and become drug addicts.

Cloward & Ohlin's ideas have been criticised, because the three types frequently blur together; for example, many people say Yardies are not an organised Criminal structure but a disorganised Conflict structure. All three types might use drugs and fight over turf.

Like most Functionalist theories, Cloward & Ohlin don't explore *why* working class males are denied access to legitimate opportunities or why only a minority of working class males join these illegitimate opportunity structures instead. They don't explain why women, who are also denied opportunities, aren't more involved in crime.

GANG SUBCULTURES

A gang is any group of young people who socialise together support each other; many of these gangs are perfectly law-abiding. Socialists are more interested in deviant gangs who cause trouble in the community.

Cloward & Ohlin define a gang as a **Conflict Subculture** that is less organised than a **Criminal Subculture**. Gangs could be seen as a midway point between loosely organised **Delinquent Subcultures** and professionally organised criminal ones. Gangs have rules for admittance, a loose hierarchy (or at least a leader) and usually have membership rituals, a uniform and a name.

AO2 ILLUSTRATION: *COMANDO VERMELHO*

Comando Vermelho (Red Commando) is the oldest Brazilian gang based in a favela named Antares on the outskirts of Rio De Janeiro. It was formed in the 1970s by a mixture of convicts and Communist activists, although it has lost its political identity. In the early 2000s, it fought several small-scale conflicts with the rival gang *Terceiro Comando* but went on to fight a battle with the police in 2007 where 27 people died.

The favelas are slums built around Rio De Janeiro, largely controlled by gangs. *Comando Vermelho* recruits young recruits by sponsoring sports and music events. Brazilian *funk* is a style of music and the gang funds music studio to produce and sell songs and play them on pirate radio stations. The songs advertise the gang and celebrate its dead members.

Comando Vermelho doesn't have a strict hierarchy; it's made up of cells, each with its own leader. In some ways it is more like a criminal organisation than a gang; in other ways, it resembles a private army.

Research: Watch the film *City of God* (dir. Meirelles & Lund, 2002) or *Ross Kemp On Gangs* (*Rio De Janeiro*, 2005), both of which feature Comando Vermelho; research more about the favellas and the gangs there

RESEARCH PROFILE: PATRICK (1973)

James Patrick (a pseudonym, not his real name) is a Scottish sociologist who, in 1966 and aged 23, infiltrated the **Young Team**, a street gang in Maryhill, Glasgow. Patrick had befriended a gang leader, Tim Molloy (also not his real name) who vouched for him to the rest of the gang and protected Patrick's identity.

Patrick dressed in the style of the gang (with the top button of his jacket fastened) but did not carry a knife as the others did. He only pretended to take drugs when they did.

Patrick spent 4 months with the gang, meeting the 12 times and making 120 hours of observations. He held back when the Young Team had a fight with the rival Barnes Road Gang. This aroused the suspicions of Dave, another gang member. Although Tim tried to protect him, Patrick ended the research and left the gang before a fight with Dave became inevitable.

Patrick wrote up all his notes from memory afterwards. He published them as *A Glasgow Gang Observed* (1973). He delayed publishing to protect the safety of gang members like Tim from reprisals. He never revealed his own identity to protect himself from the gang seeking revenge for betraying their trust.

The research demonstrates the violence of gangs and also their loose hierarchical structure and precise dress codes.

*Patrick's study is a **participant observation**, where he joined the group he was studying and took part in its activities. It is a **covert observation** because the other members did not realise Patrick was observing them. These concepts will be important when you study **2A: Research Methods**.*

ANTI-SCHOOL SUBCULTURES

A deviant subculture that falls short of delinquency (but sometimes overlaps with it) is the Anti-School Subculture. This is a sub-group of teenagers who reject educational attainment as a goal. They might truant from school and, in classes, disrupt lessons or simply refuse to work. These students are not deterred by school punishments and may even take some pride in being punished.

Outside of school, these young people may or may not be **delinquent** or involved in Criminal Subcultures. Many are perfectly well-behaved outside of school: they want to work and earn money, but not sit exams and do homework.

Playing truant on the Thames (photo: pily pily)

AO2 ILLUSTRATION: TRUANTING

Officially, the unexcused absence rate in all schools in England is around 1.4%. This amounts to two and half days during the academic year. However, the charity **Family Lives** estimates 64,000 pupils skip school every day and not all of these get recorded as unauthorised. The 1996 Education Act means parents pay a £60 fine if their child truants and a court can impose a £2,500 fine for persistent truanting. Only 13% of persistent truants achieved 5+ GCSEs at level 4+ compared to 60% among non-truants. Persistent absenteeism has also been linked to crime, teenage pregnancy and drug abuse. Truants are more likely to suffer from unemployment and social isolation: "*Children who miss school, miss out as adults*" (**Nick Gibb, 2012**).

Ensuring young people stay in school is important for social order, both because they are less able to carry out crime or delinquency right now and they're less likely to have social problems for years afterwards. However, young people sometimes miss school to escape bullying, because they need to work or because they are carers at home. Not all truanting is linked to poverty: in 2016, Bath & North East Somerset had one of the highest levels of truancy despite being one of the wealthiest districts.

RESEARCH PROFILE: COHEN (1955)

Albert Cohen (don't confuse him with Stan Cohen, p56) wrote *Delinquent Boys* **(1955)**. Cohen is a Functionalist who thinks that everyone learns the same values through socialisation, so working class youths have the same goals in life as middle class youths.

Cohen argues that students always seek **status** (respect, praise, success). Working class students cannot compete with their middle class peers. They experience **status frustration**. Rather than accept their inferior status, they form a deviant subculture which 'flips' mainstream norms and values. This means things that were good (like handing in homework and following the rules) become 'bad' and things that were bad (like destroying school property and getting punished by teachers) become 'good.' Now the anti-school students have status in their own eyes.

In some ways this is like **Miller**'s **Focal Concerns** (p39), but Cohen insists the deviant working class youths start off socialised into society's **value consensus**, but then they rebel against it.

Paul Willis' study of 'the Lads' (*c.f.* **1A: Socialisation, Culture & Identity**) is in opposition to Cohen's ideas. Willis claims that 'the Lads' never had any interest in 'becoming middle class' or succeeding at school. They weren't 'frustrated' because education never offered them anything they cared about.

Cohen only discusses boys (a problem shared by many **Neo-Marxists** who criticise his ideas) and fails to address the inequalities of the wider Capitalist society working class boys live in.

SPECTACULAR YOUTH SUBCULTURES

This is a term used by sociologists to describe some of the British Youth Subcultures of the 1950s, '60 and '70s, including **Teddy Boys** (p43), **Mods** (p29), **Skinheads** (p28) and **Punks**. These subcultures were visually distinctive in the way they dressed and confrontational in their attitudes to outsiders. They were associated with music genres that inspired them. **Goths** (p36) would also count as a Spectacular Youth Subculture that emerged in the 1980s but they are less political and working class than the earlier subcultures.

Punks (photo: agogo)

AO2 ILLUSTRATION: PUNKS (continued)

Punk appeared in the late 1970s. Punks adopted a shocking look, with brightly coloured hair shaved or shaped into spikes or fins; makeup was aggressive, often with facial piercings; clothing was torn leather, denim and plastic, often recycled from second-hand items. Punk celebrated anti-authority, do-it-yourself values.

There was cross-dressing among Punks, such as men wearing ripped-up skirts, fishnet tights and excessive makeup, or women with shaved heads wearing denim jackets and combat boots. This made Punk popular with young women, despite its values of masculine strength and anger.

Punk music (typified by **The Sex Pistols**) celebrated anarchy, causing offence and aggression. During the Queen's Silver Jubilee in 1977, the Six Pistols had a Number 1 hit with their mocking version of *God Save The Queen*, which was banned by the BBC for comparing the royal family to *"a fascist regime."*

RESEARCH PROFILE: HEBDIGE (1979, cont'd)

Dick Hebdige studied Punks as part of the **CCCS** (p22) and wrote *Subculture: The Meaning of Style* **(1979)**. Hebdige used the term '**bricolage**' to describe Punk culture, referring to the way it found new uses for old objects, giving them new meaning, such as dresses made from bin liners and piercings from safety pins. Punks often combined these with unexpected objects such as sexual bondage gear and swastikas. Hebdige argues that punks set out deliberately to shock mainstream society.

Hebdige argues that all subcultures develop in a similar way: (1) they form out of **resistance** to hegemony, (2) mainstream society sees these groups as deviant, leading to **fear and anxiety** about them, (3) this increases the **subculture's resistant power** but only temporarily, (4) **incorporation**, which is when business **commodify** the style of the subculture (turn it into a product for anyone to buy), (5) the subculture's fashion and music become available to the mainstream in a safe non-threatening form (as part of **Consumer Culture**), (6) the **resistant power** of the subculture begins to **die**.

Hebdige explains the 'life cycle' of Punk but he is criticised for ignoring American Punk, which started earlier than the UK scene and lasted long, with different values and not related to the UK class system.

Research: revisit your notes on **1A: Socialisation, Culture & Identity** and combine these ideas with the details on Punk as part of **social control**

PATTERNS & TRENDS

According to the **Joseph Rowntree Foundation (JRF)** more than 4/10 males and 1/10 females are likely to be found guilty or cautioned for an offence at some point during their lives. However, only about 5% of males are **chronic offenders** who account for about half of all known offending. The pattern of lifelong offending seems to begin in youth.

According to the **Ministry of Justice (2019)** the number of children who received a caution or sentence has fallen by 83% over the last ten years.

PATTERNS & TRENDS: SOCIAL CLASS

According to **National Prison Survey (2020)**, 41% of male convicts come from unskilled or skilled manual classes. According to the **Mayor of London's Office (2019)**, three-quarters of the boroughs in London with the highest levels of violent offending are also in the top 10 most deprived, while the same boroughs also have higher proportions of children living in poverty than the London average. This certainly links crime to deprivation and low social class.

However, these figures can be misleading. Prison surveys only include people caught and convicted and given prison sentences; wealthier and better educated criminals (including **white collar criminals**) are more likely to escape detection, more able to afford good lawyers and less likely to be given prison sentences for their 'victimless' crimes.

Chambliss' Saints & Roughnecks study (p19) shows that children from middle class backgrounds are treated differently by the agencies of social control, are less likely to be labelled negatively and can get away with offences that poorer people cannot.

The Prison Reform Trust (2010) reports that 2000-3000 children are in custody at any time. A survey of 200 young people in custody found half came from deprived backgrounds and three-quarters had absent fathers; another common factor was exclusion from school or regular **truanting** (p47). This suggests the issue is more complicated than just 'social class,' with several factors combining to draw youngsters into crime.

AO2 ILLUSTRATION: THE 2011 LONDON RIOTS

In the summer of 2011, there was a week of rioting in towns and cities across England, but largely in London and starting in Tottenham. TV viewers were shocked to see battles with the police, the burning of cars, buses and shops as well as looting on a huge scale. There were 5 deaths and over £200 million in property damage.

The police made over 3000 arrests and courts had to open for extended hours to process all the cases. An instruction came from the Conservative Government that rioter be punished with strong sentences, including 4 years for a man who stayed home but encouraged rioting via Facebook.

While 12% of the working-age population of the UK are on benefits of some sort, 35% of the adults prosecuted after the riots were on benefits. Some commentators took this as evidence for the link between class and crime – or for the **New Right**'s idea of the crime-prone **underclass** (38).

London riots (photo: StuartBannock)

PATTERNS & TRENDS: GENDER

According to the **Ministry of Justice (2019)**, 85% of children receiving a caution or a sentence were boys (51% of the population), but girls accounted for 15% (49% of the population).

This certainly supports the idea that males are more deviant and criminal then females. It is tied to the **Feminist** observation that young women experience more **social control** and have to enact their resistance as part of **bedroom culture** (p30) rather than in public, which would explain why they are not arrested by the police.

A different argument is the **Chivalry Theory**, which suggests that, because girls are stereotyped as more fragile and innocent than boys, they are more likely to be ignored, released or let of with warnings rather than arrested.

The Youth Justice Board (2009) shows that the peak age for female offending is 15, but it is 18 for males. This suggests that females start deviant behaviour earlier (but perhaps with less serious transgressions) then grow out of it, whereas male deviance continues into their 20s with much more serious consequences.

AO2 ILLUSTRATION: THE 2011 LONDON RIOTS

While 49% of the population of the UK in 2011 were male, 90% of the adults prosecuted after the riots were male. Some commentators took this as evidence for the link between males and crime.

PATTERNS & TRENDS: ETHNICITY

According to the **Ministry of Justice (2019)**, 69% of arrests of 10-17 year olds were of White children (84% of the population), arrests of Black children accounted for 16% (5% of the population), arrests of Asian children made up 6% of the total (9% of the population). This shows that, as a proportion of the population, more Black young people are being arrested, but less White youths. However, it should be noted that arrest rates have been falling for **all** ethnic groups over the last 10 years, but for White youths the fall has been faster, widening this gap.

These official figures need to be considered in the light of accusations of **institutional or systemic racism** (*c.f.* **1A: Socialisation, Culture & Identity**). The police might be more likely to stop and search Black youths, more like to arrest them if they see something suspicious and courts might be more likely to convict them of offences. **Geoff Pearson & Mike Rowe (2020)** spent 7 years observing UK police officers carrying out stop & search and conclude its use with Black suspects is disproportionate.

The idea of **secondary deviance** (p42) and **Hall's study of racist moral panics in the news** (p40) should remind you that ordinary witnesses might be more likely to interpret Black youths as behaving suspiciously and be more likely to call the police than they would be for White youths doing the same things.

AO2 ILLUSTRATION: THE 2011 LONDON RIOTS (cont'd)

While 3% of the population of the UK in 2011 was Black – rising to 11% in London as a whole – 50% of the adults prosecuted after the riots were Black. Some commentators took this as evidence for the link between ethnicity and crime – or for the **Neo-Marxist** idea of the police targeting Black working class people disproportionately.

EXAM PRACTICE: DEVIANT SUBCULTURES

The OCR exam has three questions in **Paper 1 Section B**. Questions 4-6 are on Families & Relationships and questions 10-12 are on the Media, but this Study Guide is focused on Option 2, which contains questions 7-9:

7. Outline two types of deviant youth subculture. **[12 marks: 8 AO1 + 4 AO2]**

This is very similar to Q2 in Section A, but with no source A and B; you get more marks for knowledge of Sociology here and far fewer for real life illustrations.

Choose two types of deviant subculture – perhaps anti-school and spectacular or else gangs and criminals. It's a good idea to refer to named sociologists (like Cloward & Ohlin or Cohen) and you should definitely use some sociological terminology (like opportunity structures, resistance, social control). Then offer examples of subculture and make sure each example has an explanation of **why** *it is deviant. For example, "Punks because their body piercings and outrageous hairstyle shocked ordinary people in the 1970s."*

8. Explain and briefly evaluate the view that youth deviance is related to gender. **[16 marks: 8 AO1 + 4 AO2 + 4 AO3]**

This is similar to Q3 in Section A, but with fewer marks given to AO2 illustration.

Write three paragraphs. Each paragraph should introduce a sociological idea with some illustration from the real world. Each paragraph should finish off with a brief evaluation. For example, you could write about the different ages males and females peak for offending, then the different crime rates for young men and women, then finish off with **McRobbie & Garber's idea of bedroom culture** *(p30).*

9. Assess the New Right explanation of youth deviance. **[24 marks: 8 AO1 + 8 AO2 + 8 AO3]**

This is a question with equal weight given to knowledge of Sociology, illustration and evaluation. The evaluation has to be developed evaluation; see **Chapter 5** *for advice on this.*

Write three paragraphs. Each paragraph should introduce a sociological idea with some illustration from the real world. Each paragraph should finish off with a developed evaluation. For example, you could write about the idea of single parent families not socialising their children properly, then worklessness making young men irresponsible and delinquent, then finish off with **Murray's argument that this underclass is caused by the 'benefits trap' (p38)**.

CHAPTER FOUR – DEVIANCE & THE MEDIA

The Media refers to any type of mass communication, from billboards to those flyers that come through your door offering free pizzas. Here it particularly refers to the news media (newspapers, magazines, TV and radio news, Internet news services) that reports youth deviance.

It's important to remember that the news media is carefully selected (or 'curated'). Most things that happen never get reported: no matter how important they might be for individuals, they're not considered 'news' by the media companies that publish the news. In this case, there are daily incidents of youth deviance (children truant school, two gangs fight, teenagers steal from a shop) that never make the news, though it causes distress to parents, neighbours and shopkeepers.

News is selected in accordance with 'news values.' These include things like **frequency** and **timeliness** (is the incident happening a lot and is it recent?) but also **conflict** and **negativity** (dramatic conflict is interesting and bad news is better than good news) along with **unambiguity** (is it clear who the good guys and bad guys are?).

News values were summed up by American publisher **William Randolph Hearst** in the 1890s: "*If it bleeds, it leads*." Hearst meant that sensationalist stories of violence and death would always make the front page.

News values influence the way a story is presented: the headline that accompanies it, the choice of wording, the pictures that are used, all chosen to manipulate the audience to respond in a certain way.

Positive Views of the Media

The news media brings us knowledge of what's ging on in the world. It educates us about our society, which is far too large and complicated for us to understand just based on our own social contacts and personal experiences.

More importantly, the news media alerts us to rising threats to our way of life, whether it is crime or political corruption or foreign threats. The news media helps define and sometimes change our shared values. People commonly discuss the news over their tea or coffee breaks. How they react to provocative storis helps set the boundaries of acceptable behaviour; when people come together in shock and outrage, their experience social solidity (a sense of belonging).

The news media also has a role in evolving our shared values. Newspapers run campaigns to reform the law. For example, after a series of knife attacks, the *Daily Express* ran a campaign in 2009 to ban the sale of 'Zombie Knives' (large, stylish weapons based on the knives in video games).

This is a **Functionalist** view of the news. It is based on a **pluralist view of the media**: news companies are driven by profit and deliver the content people want to watch and read; they are not able to control us and instead we the consumers have control over them.

Negative Views of the Media

A different view of the news media is that it distorts our understanding of what is happening in society, promoting fear and outrage. The newspapers in the UK tend to be Right Wing and their campaigns are often to have things banned and to resist the rights of minority groups.

For example, back in 1986 *The Sun* ran a campaign to remove homosexual literature from school libraries, based around a book called *Jenny Lives With Eric & Martin*, supposedly available to children and featuring same-sex parenting. *The Sun* called this a 'direct threat to the nation's children' and the Conservative Government introduced Clause 28 in 1988, banning the 'promotion' of homosexuality in schools (including sex education teaching about homosexuality).

Marxists claim that news stories are curated to support **hegemonic power**, by presenting non-hegemonic groups (e.g. the working classes, ethnic minorities, homosexuals) as threats. The **Marxist instrumentalist view** is that newspapers are owned by 'press barons' who are in league with the ruling classes and manipulate their audiences to be submissive. The **Neo-Marxist view** is that journalists are reasonably independent but still get hired because their views match the owners and editors and don't want to stray too far from the hegemonic line in case they get fired.

Feminists similarly see the news media as promoting patriarchy, with stories that **objectify women** (focusing on their bodies and shaming them for their imperfections) and only showing them in a narrow range of stereotypical roles.

Research: revisit your notes on **1A: Socialisation, Culture & Identity** and combine these ideas with the details about Rupert Murdoch's News Corporation and Clause 28

AO2 ILLUSTRATION: THE 1964 SEASIDE RIOTS

In 1964, two new Youth Subcultures had emerged in the UK. The Mods were largely working class, but valued a smart and stylish appearance and drove scooters. The Rockers tended to be from more middle class homes, but preferred a long-haired look, wearing leather jackets and driving motorbikes. The two groups had little to do with each other, following different bands and pursuing different lifestyles.

But in the Easter of 1964, young Londoners descended on the seaside resort of Clacton, enjoying the mobility their motorbikes and scooters. Fights broke out, with scuffles on the promenade and stone-throwing. There were 64 arrests.

On Easter Monday, the newspapers had headlines like *'Day of Terror by Scooter Groups'* (*Daily Telegraph*) and *'Youngsters Beat Up Town - 97 Leather Jacket Arrests'* (*Daily Express*).

After that reporting, newspaper readers waited anxiously for the next Bank Holiday in May. Thousands of Mods and Rockers descended on Brighton, Clacton, Margate and other resorts, all expecting trouble. The police were there in force. Journalists were there too, taking photographs of the fighting. The headlines reported *'The Battle of Brighton'* (1000 youths involved and 76 arrests). Newspaper editorials predicted the collapse of society, referring to the youths as *'vermin'* and *'mutated locusts wreaking untold havoc on the land'*.

RESEARCH PROFILE: COHEN (1972)

Stan Cohen (1942–2013 and not to be confused with Albert Cohen the Functionalist, p48) wrote a classic in media studies, *Folk Devils & Moral Panics* **(1972)**.

Cohen researched the fights which took place in English seaside resorts on Bank Holidays in 1964 between two youth subcultures: the **Mods** (p29) and the motorbike-riding **Rockers**.

Cohen was an **Interactionist** (p11) influenced by **Becker's Labelling Theory**. He was more interested in the way newspapers reported the events than rather than the events themselves. His study was a mixture of observation, content analysis (looking at the language and images of the 1964 news reports) and interviews.

Cohen concludes that the media reporting was very different from the actual events, but it had a huge influence on the subsequent behaviour of the two sets of youths and the police. In effect, the Media *created* the deviance rather than just reporting it.

Cohen suggested that there are five groups involved in the process of moral panic. There is the **threat** that starts the moral panic, which Cohen calls a "**folk devil**." There are **enforcers of laws**, like the police. There is the **news media** reporting on it and attaching symbolic images to it. There are **politicians**, who sometimes add to the panic. Finally, there is **the public**, which becomes concerned about the threat and demands something be done about it.

DEVIANCE & THE MEDIA: A TOOLKIT

Most of this part of the course draws on **Cohen (1972)** and the ideas in *Folk-Devils & Moral Panics*.

The idea of the Media *causing* deviancy depends on the **Hypodermic Syringe Model** of media influence, which assumes that the Media can 'inject' ideas into its audience and manipulate their behaviour. This in turn assumes that audiences are completely passive, unable to tell truth from fiction and blindly accept what they are told.

Most sociologists reject the Hypodermic Syringe Model as too simplistic. They prefer various **Active Audience Models** that propose that people pick and choose what to pay attention to and what to believe from the Media.

This still leaves a big question about whether a moral panic in the Media really can change the way people think and behave – or whether those changes were about to happen anyway and the Media just happened to be around to report on it. **Cohen's theory** credits the Media with a lot of influence (and Marxist variations on it tend to credit the Media with even more power to control us), but critics point out that a lot of people never read or watch the news and, if they do, they only pay attention to the bits that interest them, like sport. *How many people really followed the news reports of the Mods and the Rockers in 1964?*

MORAL PANICS

A **moral panic** is a widespread fear, usually an irrational one, that has been promoted by the news media. It is then fuelled by politicians and often results in new laws or policies that target a group viewed as dangerous. Moral panics often lead to increased social control.

Moral panics often target **marginalised groups** (i.e. subcultures in society or minorities) by drawing on **negative stereotypes**.

It's worth asking whether a moral panic always targets a marginalised group. This would suggest there can never be a moral panic about the behaviour of politicians or celebrities or the middle classes. Is that true?

Cohen (1972) describes the moral panic over Mods and Rockers in 1964. He describes the five stages of a moral panic:

1. A group is **represented as a threat** to social norms and society at large
2. The news media presents the threat in **simplistic, symbolic ways** that the public can recognise
3. **Public concern** is aroused
4. The authorities (i.e. police, politicians) respond to the threat with **new laws or policies**
5. This leads to **social change** in the community.

Goode & Ben-Yehuda (1994) add more elements of a moral panic, including the idea that it should be **disproportionate** (public concern is greater than the threat deserves) and **volatile** (public interest moves on and the moral panic is forgotten about).

AO2 ILLUSTRATION: RECENT MORAL PANICS

Moral panics didn't end in 1964. You have already read about *The Sun* leading a moral panic about homosexuality in schools in 1986 which led to the passage of Clause 28, a classic example of a panic leading to social change. This moral panic coincided with the appearance of the disease AIDS among the homosexual community, so the newspaper focusing on *Jenny Lives With Eric & Martin* was a simplistic, symbolic way of presenting a complicated threat.

After the **9/11 bombing** in 2001, **Islamophobia** became a moral panic, leading to the invasions of Afghanistan and Iraq – the most dramatic sort of new policy and social change imaginable. Images of the burning World Trade Centre towers became a simplistic, symbolic way of presenting the threat.

More recently, moral panics have focused on an **'epidemic' of knife crime** among youth gangs, often linked to single parent families raising 'feral' children and Drill rap music. Photographs of the grisly knives or quotes of Drill lyrics celebrating violence are a simplistic, symbolic way of presenting the threat. This has led to calls to increase the use of police stop & search and stronger sentences for carrying a knife, as well as banning the sale of 'Zombie Knives.'

Research: research more moral panics: crack cocaine, paedophiles, violent video games, the Momo Challenge, football hooligans (especially after Euro 2020), Satanic Ritual Abuse, benefits cheats, illegal immigrants, *Dungeons & Dragons*

FOLK DEVILS

Cohen (1972) argues that when the news media reports on deviant behaviour they construct a narrative with a clear villain: he calls this the **folk devil**. In Cohen's study, the folk devils were the Youth Subcultures of **the Mods and the Rockers**. Creating a folk devil is necessary to start a moral panic.

Cohen claims there are 3 stages to the creation of a folk devil:

1. **Symbolisation:** the folk devil is oversimplified to make them easily recognizable (such as leather-clad Rockers)
2. **Exaggeration:** the facts are distorted (or even invented) to make the threat seem greater (news reporting ignored how small the groups of Mods and Rockers were)
3. **Prediction**: the threat posed by the folk devil is represented to be growing (the reporting after Easter predicted more violence at the May Bank Holiday)

Step 2 (**Exaggeration**) is the controversial part of this theory. Critics point out that some folk devils really are engaged in destructive activities and by drawing our attention to it the news media are performing a public service. For example, the **New Right** (p38) thinks that the **underclass** is a real problem, not a media exaggeration. However, the entire New Right Perspective could be criticised for being one big moral panic.

Cohen is an **Interactionist** and doesn't speculate about why some groups are targeted as folk devils but not others. **Neo-Marxists** like **Stuart Hall (1978, p40)** have an answer to this: they are **non-hegemonic groups** and they serve as a distraction from more serious problems. Hall points out that the British press made a folk devil out of Black Muggers (and by extension, all Black working class people) to cover up an economic crisis in the 1970s.

Functionalists would go further, arguing that society *needs* folk devils to define the boundaries of acceptable behaviour, reinforce (or evolve) **shared values** and promote **social solidity**. Small groups of people get stigmatised so that this can happen, but that's like having to break eggs to make an omelette. Critics find this view to be disturbingly hard-hearted.

AO2 ILLUSTRATION: RECENT FOLK DEVILS

The moral panic over Islamist terrorism has made Muslims into folk devils, but particularly Muslim women, with campaigns against the face-covering burqa (technically, it's the **niqab**, but 'burqa' seems to have stuck with the public) particularly targeting them. When France banned the wearing of the niqab in public in 2011, **Siobhan Mullally (2011)** suggested that 1900 Muslim women wore it out of a population of 4.7 million French Muslims: 0.04% and that is considered to be an over-estimate. Why such trouble over such a small group? The 'burqa' is a very recognisable image: it oversimplifies a threat in an easily recognisable way.

You have read about *The Sun*'s campaign in the 1980s which made a folk devil out of homosexuals. The story book about a girl with same-sex parents was actually found in a teachers' resource library, not a library used by pupils, but this was not made clear in the reporting. At that time, there was already a lot of fear about homosexuality because of the appearance of AIDS. Homosexuals are a non-hegemonic group (because heteronormativity is mainstream) and AIDS was identified in the 1980s news media as 'the Gay Plague.'

20,000 ARE INFECTED . . . AND IT'S GETTING WORSE

Britain threatened by gay virus plague

DEVIANCY AMPLIFICATION

Cohen (1972) borrows a concept from another Interactionist, **Leslie Wilkins (1964)**, of the **deviancy amplification spiral**.

Deviancy amplification is a type of **secondary deviance** (p42) that occurs when **formal agencies of social control** form a big part of the social reaction to deviance – when **labels** are applied by the news media, rather than just your friends and neighbours. Because the news media simplifies and exaggerates, the label it applies is much more negative that the original transgression deserves but also harder to negotiate or remove.

Deviancy amplification becomes a **'spiral'** when police and journalists go looking for more examples of the deviancy. Of course, they find it (or interpret ordinary behaviour as deviant), which adds to the perception that deviancy is increasing and getting out of control. This leads to more arrests and courts passing tougher sentences, which creates the impression of a 'crime wave.'

The **Self-Fulfilling Prophecy (SFP)** means that people accept and internalise the labels the media use. For example, in 1964 Mods and Rockers started genuinely hating each other because of the news media reporting these battles, whereas the first scuffles in Clacton only occurred because the bad weather ruined their holiday and they were bored.

Another ingredient in deviancy amplification is the work of **moral entrepreneurs (Becker, 1963)**. These are people outside of the news media who are pushing for new policies or social change. They are often politicians, but they can also be church groups, celebrities or charities. Moral entrepreneurs 'latch onto' a moral panic and do their best to fuel public concern.

Marxists point out that the deviancy amplification spiral often serves the interests of the ruling class or hegemony and justifies the use of what **Althusser** calls the **Repressive State Apparatus** (**RSA**, e.g. a police crack-down).

Sometimes moral entrepreneurs campaign for non-hegemonic groups, such as LGBT groups, ethnic minorities or women. The **2021 murder of Sarah Everard** triggered a moral panic about predatory males and violence against women, with moral entrepreneurs calling for policies like a night-time curfew for men. However, if we use **Goode & Ben-Yehuda's criterion of disproportionality** (p58), then this might *not* be a true moral panic if the threat to women from predatory men is proportionate to the public concern.

AO2 ILLUSTRATION: RECENT MORAL ENTREPRENEURS

One of the most famous moral entrepreneurs in **Mary Whitehouse** (1910-2001). Whitehouse was a teacher and a Christian who was disturbed by changes in British society, especially the sex and violence in the Media. She founded the *Clean Up TV* campaign in 1964 which became the **National Viewers & Listeners Association (NVLA)** in 1965; it became *Mediawatch-UK* in 2001.

Whitehouse campaigned against sex, nudity and violence, swearing and homosexuality in TV, pop music and news reporting. She particularly opposed violence in children's TV and criticised *Doctor Who* for this. She also opposed pornography, especially child pornography before it was widely understood to be a problem.

More recently, moral panics about Islamist terrorism and the 'burqa' have been supported by a moral entrepreneur named **Tommy Robinson**. Robinson co-founded the **English Defence League (EDL)** in 2009 to campaign against the dangers of 'radical Islam.' Robinson has been to prison several times and banned from social media platforms for promoting Hate Speech, but insists he is not against Muslims in general.

RESEARCH PROFILE: FAWBERT (2008)

Jack Fawbert wrote *Hoodies: Folk Devils and a Moral Panic for the New Millennium?* (2008) after carrying out a detailed content analysis of newspaper reports about **delinquency** between 2004 and 2008. He found only one article in 2004 that used the word 'hoodie' to describe a delinquent youth.

However, a year later, the **Bluewater Shopping Centre** banned shoppers who wore hoodies and Prime Minister **Tony Blair** promised to clamp down on anti-social behaviour by 'hoodies.' The news media seized on the term 'hoodies' between 2005 and 2007, to describe a deviant Youth Subculture. Fawbert notes that 'Hoodie' would sometimes appear in the headline, but there would be no reference in the story about whether the young criminal was actually wearing one.

This fits the description of a **moral panic**, with a social threat being represented in a simplistic and symbolic way. The Hoodie became a **folk devil**, with facts being exaggerated or even invented. The shopping centre is an example of **social change** as a result. Tony Blair is a **moral entrepreneur** entering the debate and calling for **new policies and punishments**.

Sales of hoodies soared as young people realised they upset people in authority by wearing them. This shows the **deviancy amplification spiral**, as more 'Hoodies' appear.

Banksy's Hoodie With A Knife

EXAM PRACTICE: DEVIANT SUBCULTURES

The OCR exam has three questions in **Paper 1 Section B**. Questions 4-6 are on Families & Relationships and questions 10-12 are on the Media, but this Study Guide is focused on Option 2, which contains questions 7-9:

7. Outline two folk devils in the UK media. **[12 marks: 8 AO1 + 4 AO2]**

This is very similar to Q2 in Section A, but with no source A and B; you get more marks for knowledge of Sociology here and far fewer for real life illustrations.

*Choose two folk devils to outline – probably the Mods/Rockers from 1964 and Hoodies more recently. It's a good idea to refer to named sociologists (like Cohen and Fawbert) and you should definitely use some sociological terminology (like moral panics, symbolisation, non-hegemonic groups). Then offer examples and make sure each example has an explanation of **why** it is folk devil. For example, "Mods & Rockers were made out to be a threat to the public even though the skirmishes in Clacton were not serious and only happened because the holidaying teenagers were bored."*

8. Explain and briefly evaluate the view that deviancy amplification causes deviant behaviour. **[16 marks: 8 AO1 + 4 AO2 + 4 AO3]**

This is similar to Q3 in Section A, but with fewer marks given to AO2 illustration.

*Write three paragraphs. Each paragraph should introduce a sociological idea with some illustration from the real world. Each paragraph should finish off with a brief evaluation. For example, you could write about **secondary deviance**, the **spiral** and **moral entrepreneurs**.*

9. Assess moral panics as an explanation of youth deviancy. **[24 marks: 8 AO1 + 8 AO2 + 8 AO3]**

*This is a question with equal weight given to knowledge of Sociology, illustration and evaluation. The evaluation has to be developed evaluation; see **Chapter 6** for advice on this.*

Write three paragraphs. Each paragraph should introduce a sociological idea with some illustration from the real world. Each paragraph should finish off with a developed evaluation. For example, you could write about the idea of a folk devil being identified as a threat, the media exaggerating and using simplified and symbolic images and the resulting new policies and social change. The differing views of Functionalists, the New Right and Marxists could all come into this as well as the question about whether the moral panic actually causes deviancy.

CHAPTER FIVE – EVALUATION

In **Paper 1 Section B (Option 2: Youth Subcultures)**, question 8 assesses **AO3**/evaluation and the instruction is to *"briefly evaluate"* while question 9 asks for a developed evaluation.

'Brief evaluation' does not have to be developed or address theoretical issues. It can be a common-sense comment. It should be a simple **strength**, **weakness** or **comparison**.

A developed evaluation needs to address theoretical or methodological issues. It needs to go deeper than a 'brief evaluation' and look at an issue from alternative perspectives or work through the implications of a viewpoint.

As well as the evaluative points you can find in the preceding chapters, here are some evaluative positions candidates can adopt:

Brief Evaluations

These points are suitable for Q8. You can use them in Q9 as well, but their simplicity makes them hard to turn into developed points, so you might miss out on the higher AO3 band marks. Still, better to write something than nothing at all.

"Not all people…" / Over-generalising

Structuralist Perspectives (like **Functionalism** or traditional **Marxism** and **Feminism**) are particularly prone to sweeping generalisations. They often claim that everyone is motivated by the same thing or experiences the same oppression or wants the same outcomes. For example, Functionalists claim everyone shares the same basic values in society and Feminists claim all women are in some way oppressed.

To evaluate these ideas, point out that not all people fit into this mould. Not all Punks are resisting Capitalism (p49), not all teenage girls socialise in their bedrooms (p30) and not all working class boys are frustrated in school (p48).

If you are writing about some empirical research, point out that its sample group doesn't resemble everyone. Not all delinquent schoolboys are white like the ones that William Chambliss studied (p19).

It's important not to be formulaic. Say *why* not all people are like this: give an example of one of the exceptions. Not all Punks are resisting Capitalism, because some people were only Punks *because they liked the music*. Not all delinquent schoolboys are like Chambliss' schoolboys *because some are Black or Asian and they have their own problems with racism*.

"It's out-of-date…" / Time-locked

You will probably have noticed that an awful lot of sociological research comes from the 1950s, '60s and '70s. Those were important decades when a lot of ground-breaking Sociology was done. But do theories and samples from the 1970s tell us anything about the UK in the 21st century?

To evaluate these studies, point out that so much has changed. **Mass employment in factories** has ended, **equal rights for women** has arrived (at least, in principle), the UK has **become a multicultural society**, the **Internet** has transformed the way we communicate and find out about the world (this last point makes studies from the 1980s and early '90s out-of-date too).

Once again, it's important not to be formulaic. Say **why** one of these changes matters for this particular study: give an example of one of the exceptions. McRobbie & Garber's research into the bedroom culture (p30) is out-of-date *teenagers meet online now and access the Internet from their phones not their bedrooms*. Chambliss' research into the Saints & Roughnecks (p19) is out-of-date *because in the 21st century, schools and towns have CCTV to catch kids truanting or misbehaving*.

"Nature rather than nurture…" / The Nature-Nurture Debate

Sociologists tend to assume that everything is socially constructed, but it's worth remembering that biology might be playing a neglected role in human behaviour.

To evaluate these ideas, point out that a Nativist approach might be better. Rather than explain Youth Culture through social control, maybe there are innate biological changes that go on in Youth.

It would be formulaic just to say "maybe there are innate biological changes" and leave it at that. Say **why** the Nativist approach would be better: give an example of one of the benefits. Take a Nativist approach to studying Youth Culture, *because it might tell you the role testosterone places in youthful aggression in lots of different cultures*.

Developing Evaluations

These points are suitable for Q8 or Q9. Their complexity makes them suitable for turning into developed points, so you can qualify for higher AO3 band marks on Q9.

"It's a macro-perspective / Interactionist critique

Structuralist Perspectives make sweeping generalisations because they study society as a whole and focus on important institutions rather than individual people. The **Interactionist** Perspective criticises this, saying it is better to look at society 'from the bottom up' (a **micro Perspective**). The sociologist Max Weber recommends using *Verstehen* – empathic understanding – rather than focusing on big trends.

To evaluate these ideas, point out that an Interactionist approach might be better. Rather than studying Punks as a trend in society, take a micro approach and study individual Punks.

As usual, avoid being formulaic. Say *why* the micro approach would be better: give an example of one of the benefits. Take a micro approach to studying Punks, *because they will tell you why they personally are into Punk, which may or may not have anything to do with Capitalism*.

Development

If you bring in Interactionism as the solution to the problem, don't stop there. You could give examples of studies that employ this micro approach (like **Patrick** infiltrating a Glasgow gang, p46) or explain how later research incorporates aspects of the micro approach (like the way Neo-Marxism interviews punks and skinheads).

Alternatively, criticise your own improvement: discuss the drawbacks of using the micro approach (punks might lie to the interviewer, the way the Samoan girls supposedly lied to **Margaret Mead** about their sex lives, p8).

"This is similar to…" / Comparisons

Sometimes, different sociologists or different Perspectives end up saying similar things, although usually for different reasons Marxists and Feminists both agree there is propaganda and brainwashing (**ideology**) in the news and in schools. Marxists and Functionalists both agree that modern Capitalism is stressful and difficult for ordinary youngsters. Interactionists and Marxists both agree that the police treat young people with suspicion.

To evaluate these ideas, point out the similarity between the sociology you are writing about and another Perspective or research study. If you have explained that Marxists think that the news media is brainwashing, explain that Interactionists also think the news media applies labels.

As usual, don't be formulaic. Say *why* the two approaches are so similar *or* say why they are also different: give an example. Marxists and Interactionist agree on news media because they both think the news doesn't tell us the objective truth, *although Marxists think this comes from serving the ruling class* and *Interactionists focus more on how moral entrepreneurs interfere with the news*.

Development

If you think two Perspectives are similar, don't stop there. You could give examples of studies from each perspective, like **Hall**'s study of moral panics about Black muggers (p40) compared to **Cohen**'s study of Mods & Rockers (p56); or explain how later research incorporates both perspectives, like the Neo-Marxists in the CCCS using Interactionist techniques.

Alternatively, criticise the very similarity you suggested: discuss the how differences between the two approaches are more important than similarities (Marxists recognise the overall social context of Capitalism, whereas Interactionists look at each social situation separately and miss out on the big picture).

"A Postmodernist would say ..." / Postmodern critique

Postmodernism (p12) makes a powerful criticism of other Perspectives in research from the 1990s or the 21st century.

Postmodernism proposes the big structuralists theories (Functionalism, traditional Marxism and Feminism) are meta-narratives that don't explain anything anymore. Society has become fragmented and fluid and people pick and choose aspects of their Identities. Media saturation has taken place and the difference between media image and reality has broken down.

In order to avoid being formulaic, say *why* a Postmodernist approach would be better: give an example of the benefits. Take a Postmodern approach to studying the Youth Subcultures, *because it will focus on how young people shift fluidly between different styles rather than being loyal to just one subculture.*

Development

If you think Postmodernism is good, don't stop there. You could give examples of studies from the Postmodernist perspective (like **Bennett**'s study of Newcastle clubbers, p33) or explain how Postmodernism incorporates other perspectives (like an awareness of how Capitalism affects people through advertising and branded images which is something Marxists agree with).

Alternatively, criticise the Postmodernist idea you suggested: discuss the flaws with Postmodernism (like the continued existence of subcultures like Goths, the influence the class system continues to have or the degree to which ordinary people live most of their lives offline).

"A weakness of this Perspective is ..." / Standard theoretical critiques

Functionalism

Functionalism ignores diversity: Functionalism assumes we are all the same and want the same things, but the things it says we all want tend to be the sort of things that the white middle classes want. Functionalism doesn't take seriously the idea that ethnic minorities, the working class or women might have different goals and values.

Functionalism ignores social injustice: Functionalism assumes that society is harmonious and **meritocratic** but it turns a blind eye to a lot of inequality, corruption and barriers to social mobility. It defends Capitalism as the best system we have discovered for making people healthy and wealthy while ignoring the huge human and environmental cost of Capitalism worldwide. It is also prepared to accept a lot of crime for the sake of consensus.

Functionalism celebrates Western superiority: Functionalists believe in the **'March of Progress'** and claim that the sort of liberal democratic nations you find in Europe, North America and Australia are the most advanced. Other societies ought to imitate them and immigrants ought to fit in. This ignores many flaws in Western societies (e.g. Capitalism, patriarchy, the 'storm & stress' of Youth which Mead argues doesn't exist in other cultures).

Functionalism overrates the biological: Functionalists believe society reflects unchangeable biological needs or 'human nature.' Critics argue there is no such thing as 'human nature' and that everything is **socially constructed**. 'Human nature' is often used to excuse youth deviance due to 'storm & stress' and the need to vent frustration.

Marxism

Marxism ignores progress: In the last 200 years, Capitalist societies have abolished slavery, set up human rights, created a welfare state and free education and healthcare for all. Marxists often talk as if this hasn't happened or as if it happened *in spite of* Capitalism. This pessimistic view of the past and the future perhaps exaggerates social injustice as much as Functionalism downplays it.

Marxism is a conspiracy theory: It's standard for Marxists to argue that the Media (especially the news), Education and the Workplace are all controlled by a sinister group of billionaires who brainwash everyone through **ideology**. This underestimates the independence of many journalists, teachers and bosses as well as the ability of ordinary people to think for themselves and work out what's true.

Marxists assume class is homogenous: *Homogenous* means 'all the same' and traditional Marxists think that all working class people share the same relationship to labour and power. However, **Neo-Marxists** (p40) are more aware of **intersecting Identities** and how behaviour is shaped by the particular circumstances.

Marxism offers no solutions: You don't have to be a Marxist to spot the Capitalism has flaws – Functionalists would admit *that*! Marxists argue that Capitalism is intrinsically rotten and destructive and it needs to be replaced rather than reformed. But replaced with what? Marxism can be accused of criticising Capitalism without offering a coherent alternative. Similarly, it identifies Youth Deviance as resistance, but doesn't suggest what can be done about it's destructive aspects.

Feminism

Feminism ignores biology: Feminists insist that gender is **socially constructed,** and it certainly is up to a point. However, Psychology reveals lots of biological differences in brain structure, hormones and genes between the sexes and it's unlikely that *none* of this makes *any* difference to social behaviour. But if Gender Identity is even partly based on unchangeable sexual differences, then some of the situations women are in might not be *entirely* due to Patriarchy.

Feminism ignores progress: In the last century women have won the vote, the right to be educated at university and manage their own affairs. In Britain, the Sexual Discrimination Act (1975) has outlawed sexual discrimination. Feminism can be accused of downplaying this progress and exaggerating the scale of injustice. However, the Sarah Everard murder can be used to show that women in the 21st century are still not safe.

Feminists assume gender is homogenous: As with Marxists and social class, traditional Feminists are accused of treating all women as if they experienced the same oppression – which in practice means assuming that the difficulties of White women are typical for all women. Clearly, young women (and especially young lesbian women) have different experiences.

Feminists ignore the oppression of men: Feminists sometimes seem to assume that Masculinity is homogenous and all men are complicit in the Patriarchy, but men are much more likely than women to die by violence, to be victims of crime and to work in dangerous conditions. Many young men are also victims of oppression and die in dangerous jobs, through violence or suicide.

Interactionism

Interactionism cannot be generalised: Because it tends to do research on small groups, studying micro relationships and beliefs, it's hard to generalise the conclusions of Interactionism to other groups or society on a macro level.

Interactionists cannot be objective: The close-up and personal nature of Interactionist research and its focus on *Verstehen* makes it very **subjective** – just a matter of opinion – whereas Sociology claims to be a social *science* that explores facts in an **objective** way.

Interactionism is an incomplete explanation: Even when Interaction identifies processes that seem to be quite generalisable – like the **Self-Fulfilling Prophecy** – its small-scale micro view means it doesn't explore where these processes come from. Marxists argue that Interactionism is incomplete as an explanation without including Capitalism and **ruling class ideology**. Functionalists would also say Interactionism needs to explain how the experiences of little groups fit into a theory of society's functions and requirements.

Postmodernism

Postmodernism ignores continuing modernity: The Internet has made huge changes to our lives, along with technology like mobile phones and satellite TV. However, life for many people continues as it did in the 1960s, '70s and '80s: they live in nuclear families, work in factories or offices, take part in religious worship and live in social classes. Only a minority of people – and perhaps, only in a few big cities – enjoys the unusual, ever-changing, online lifestyles that Postmodernism claims are typical. This is Giddens' argument for **Late Modernity** (p13).

Postmodernists reject objective truth: By rejecting **meta-narratives**, Postmodernism rejects objective truth. Nothing is absolutely and provably true, it can only ever be subjective truth (true-for-you or true-as-you-see-it). But how can social problems be solved unless we agree they objectively *are* problems? Why should sociological research be taken seriously if it's only a point of view? How can we tell good points of view from wild conspiracy theories and 'fake news'?

Postmodernism only applies to some topics: Postmodernism is great for explaining shifts in style and fashion, personal Identity, consumer choice and lifestyles, especially online lifestyles. It's less good for tackling the harder topics of poverty, discrimination and violence. It **also lacks political solutions** for tackling these things. Marxism tends to inspire Left Wing (Labour) policies and Functionalism (and sometimes the New Right) inspires Right Wing (Conservative) policies, but it's difficult to see any policies that have come from Postmodernism.

The New Right

The New Right lacks empirical support: Most of the support for the New Right comes from news stories about working class deviance – but those stories might be exaggerated. Hard evidence for the existence of an **underclass** is not plentiful and there's even less evidence for a whole group of people (rather than a few individuals) who reject society's values, don't want to work, don't want to live in families and embrace crime as a lifestyle.

The New Right demonises the vulnerable: The New Right is accused of 'punching down' – targeting the group in society that most needs help and making them out to be monstrous and calling for any sort of help (in the form of benefits) to be taken away. **Marxists** find it fairly easy to characterise the New Right as a **hegemonic attack on the poor**. However, Marxists can be characterised as glamorising delinquents and criminals as noble underdogs and ignoring the damage they do in society.

The New Right exaggerates deviancy: The New Right presents the underclass as a growing problem that threatens the whole of society. Even **Functionalists** criticise this approach as alarmist. Functionalist believe that deviancy is necessary and ultimately benefits society. However, the New Right emerged partly because both Functionalists and Marxists seemed to be making excuses for crime rather than doing anything practical to put a stop to it.

Development

If you offer a theoretical weakness, don't stop there. You could give examples of studies that illustrate that weakness (like Murray's warning that single mothers are raising feral boys and promiscuous girls illustrates the New Right demonising the vulnerable). Alternatively, follow through the implications of this weakness (what would happen if politicians acted on Murray's suggestions) or bring in other Perspectives that have something to say about this weakness (like Marxists characterising the attack as serving hegemonic power).

Alternatively, criticise the weakness you suggested by arguing that it isn't really a weakness: Murray thinks the real enemies of the poor are the people who keep them in a benefits trap that appears kind but is actually dehumanising – you would be doing the underclass a favour by getting them off benefits and into family arrangements.

EXAM PRACTICE: SECTION B

The OCR exam has three questions in **Paper 1 Section B**. Questions 4-6 are on Families & Relationships and questions 10-12 are on the Media, but this Study Guide is focused on Option 2, which contains questions 7-9:

7. Outline two moral panics in the UK media. **[12 marks: 8 AO1 + 4 AO2]**

This is very similar to Q2 in Section A, but with no source A and B; you get more marks for knowledge of Sociology here and far fewer for real life illustrations.

*Choose two moral panics to outline – probably the Mods/Rockers from 1964 and Hoodies more recently. It's a good idea to refer to named sociologists (like Cohen and Fawbert) and you should definitely use some sociological terminology (like moral panics, symbolisation, non-hegemonic groups). Then offer examples and make sure each example has an explanation of **why** it is a moral panic. For example, "Mods & Rockers had a brief skirmish in Clacton but the newspapers exaggerated it into 'Day of Terror!'"*

8. Explain and briefly evaluate the view that youth deviance is related to social class. **[16 marks: 8 AO1 + 4 AO2 + 4 AO3]**

This is similar to Q3 in Section A, but with fewer marks given to AO2 illustration.

Write three paragraphs. Each paragraph should introduce a sociological idea with some illustration from the real world. Each paragraph should finish off with a brief evaluation. For example, you could write about trends in working class deviance, Marxist views on working class youth deviance and Chambliss' study of the Saints & the Roughnecks (p19).

9. Assess postmodern explanations of youth subcultures. **[24 marks: 8 AO1 + 8 AO2 + 8 AO3]**

*This is a question with equal weight given to knowledge of Sociology, illustration and evaluation. The evaluation has to be developed evaluation; see **Chapter 6** for advice on this.*

Write three paragraphs. Each paragraph should introduce a sociological idea with some illustration from the real world. Each paragraph should finish off with a developed evaluation. For example, you could write about Polhemus' idea of a supermarket of style for young people (p25), Maffesoli's idea of Neo-Tribes replacing subcultures (p33) and Postman's idea of the disappearance of childhood (p13).

KEY RESEARCH

The 20 studies here cover all the topics that arise in this Section of the exam and they will prove just as useful in later sections too. Start learning them. For each study, I include the key terms, a Perspective (if relevant) and the particular topics it is linked to.

Cashmore (1997): *The Black Culture Industry*, hybridity, Hip-Hop as a commodity; **Postmodernism**; youth subculture & ethnicity, p31

CCCS (1970s): *Resistance Through Rituals* etc.; **Neo-Marxism**; subcultures & class, deviant spectacular subcultures, p22

Chambliss (1973): *The Saints & the Roughnecks*, labelling; **Interactionism, Neo-Marxism**; youth culture, subcultures & class, deviant delinquent subcultures, p19

Clarke, Cohen (1976): *Resistance Through Rituals*, skinheads, symbolic resistance; **Neo-Marxism**; youth subcultures & class, deviant spectacular subcultures, p28

Cloward & Ohlin (1960): legitimate & illegitimate opportunity structures, criminal, conflict, retreatist; **Functionalism**; deviant criminal/gang subcultures, p45

Cohen, A (1955): *Delinquent Boys*, status frustration; **Functionalism**; deviant delinquent/anti-school subcultures, p48

Cohen, S (1972): *Folk Devils & Moral Panics*, 1964 Mods v Rockers riots; **Interactionism**; media & deviance, p56

Durkheim (1895): society of saints; **Functionalism**; youth deviance, p37

Eisenstadt (1956): *Generation To Generation*, anomie, social integration, transgression; **Functionalism**; youth culture, youth deviance, p17

Fawbert (2008): *Hoodies: Folk Devils for the New Millennium?* Moral panic over hoodies; **Interactionist**; media & deviance, p61

Hall (1978): *Policing the Crisis*, moral panic over Black muggers; **Neo-Marxism**; subculture & ethnicity, deviant delinquent subcultures, media & deviance, p40

Hebdige (1979): *Subculture: The Meaning of Style*, punks, resistance, bricolage, incorporation; **Neo-Marxism**; deviant spectacular subcultures, p49

Jefferson (1976): *Resistance Through Rituals*, Teddy Boys; **Neo-Marxism**; deviant delinquent/spectacular subcultures, p44

Maffesoli (1977): *The Time of the Tribes*, neo-tribes replace subcultures; **Postmodernism**; youth subcultures & hybridity, p33

Mead (1928): *Coming of Age in Samoa*; youth culture without Storm & Stress, p8

McRobbie & Garber (1976): *Resistance Through Rituals*, invisibility of girls, bedroom culture; **Feminism**; youth subcultures & gender, p30

Miller (1958): working class focal concerns; **Functionalism**; subcultures & class, deviant delinquent/anti-school subcultures, p39

Murray (1984): underclass; **New Right**; subcultures & class, deviant delinquent/gang subcultures, p38

Patrick (1973): *A Glasgow Gang Observed*, participant observation; **Interactionist**; deviant gang subcultures, p46

Willis (1977): *Learning to Labour*, the Lads; **Marxism**; subcultures & class, deviant anti-school subcultures, pError! Bookmark not defined.

Patterns & Trends

You also need to be able to cite some patterns and trends in youth deviance (p50):

Joseph Rowntree Foundation: 4/10 males and 1/10 females cautioned or arrested at some point; only 5% responsible for 50% of crime

Mayor of London's Office (2019): 75% of offending in top 10 most deprived areas of London

Ministry of Justice (2019): children cautioned or sentenced has fallen 83% in last 10 years; 85% are boys, 15% girls; 69% are White, 16% Black, 6% Asian (out of 84%, 5%, 9% of population)

National Prison Survey (2020): 41% of convicts from manual classes

Prison Reform Trust (2010): survey of 200 young offenders found 50% from deprived backgrounds, 75% with absent fathers; also school exclusion

Youth Justice Board (2009): peak age for female offending is 15 but 18 for males

FURTHER RESEARCH

These studies are less central to any argument. Some of them just reference a useful piece of terminology. Others offer criticism of a Key Study or are the original research that a Key Study is criticising.

Althusser (1970): RSA and ISA, p40

Baudrillard (1970): hyper-reality, p13

Becker (1963): *Outsiders*, labelling theory, p12

Bennett (1999): supports Maffesoli, p33

Brake (1980): subcultures as magical solutions, p41

Davies (1967): deviance is a safety valve, p37

Faludi (1999): *Stiffed*, delinquents obsessed with celebrity, p13

Giddens (1999): *Runaway World*, Late Modernity, p13

Goode & Ben-Yehuda (1994): adds elements to moral panics, p58

Greer (2014): critiques *Everyday Sexism Project*, p16

Hodkinson (2002): researches why Goths continue into adulthood, p36

Hollands & Chatterton (2002): youth culture is commercialised now, p32

Johal (1998): Brasians, hyper-ethnic style, p30

Lemert (1967): secondary deviance, p42

Lyotard (1979): end of meta-narratives, p13

Matza (1964): Drift Theory, subterranean values, p42

Polhemus (1997): the 'Supermarket of Style'

Postman (1994): *The Disappearance of Childhood*; breakdown of youth, p13

St Croix (2017): criticises NCS, p18

Cohen (1955): status frustration, p**Error! Bookmark not defined.**

Freeman (1983): criticises Mead (1928) p**Error! Bookmark not defined.**

Gramsci (--): introduces idea of hegemonic control to **Neo-Marxism**, 40

Hall, G S (1904): coined *'Sturm und Drang'* (Storm & Stress)

Rimmer (2010): studied Makina fans, p32

Willis (1977): *Learning To Labour*, criticises Cohen's status frustration, 48

Willis (1990): end of spectacular youth subcultures, p32

Young (1984): bulimic society, p39

GLOSSARY

Alienation: Marxist idea similar to **anomie** that workers under Capitalism become alienated from their labour and themselves by dehumanising conditions

Anomie: literally means "without norms" and it refers to the sense of disconnection and anxiety that occurs when people do not feel a connection to their society and their work; Functionalists say it is caused by the breakdown of **social solidity** and a lack of **value consensus**

Bedroom Culture: according to **McRobbie & Garber (1976)**, the way teenage girls resist hegemonic and patriarchal culture in private spaces, through the consumption of media products (e.g. teen magazines, pop music) and experimenting with appearance

Capitalism: an economic system that promotes the private ownership of property, the pursuit of profit and the concentration of wealth in the hands of a minority of people; the opposite is Communism, which abolishes private property to make everyone economically equal

CCS: Centre for Contemporary Cultural Studies at the University of Birmingham; carried out research into **Spectacular Youth Subcultures** from a **Neo-Marxist** Perspective

Culture: the set of norms and values passed on by one generation to the next, including a version of history and traditional institutions that make up a way of life; cultures vary from one society to another and change (slowly) over time

Deviance: Behaviour that goes against **norms** and **values**

Feminism: a sociological Perspective that identified conflict between the sexes; believes in a Patriarchy which subordinates women and maintains male power through coercion and violence

Folk Devil: a group identified as a threat to society during a **moral panic**

Functionalism: a sociological Perspective that promotes consensus around shared values; believes in a biological basis for human social behaviour and the inevitability of deviance

Gender: the norms and values linked to biological sex; males are often expected to behave in a masculine way and females in a feminine way: male/female are sexes but masculine/feminine are genders

Globalisation: a process going on that makes different parts of the world more interconnected through travel, global **Capitalism** and the **Mass Media**

Hegemony: the dominance of one group and their culture in society; hegemonic culture is the version of culture that commands the most respect; according to **Neo-Marxists** hegemonic culture manufactures consent

Ideology: a set of ideas and values that influence how people interpret society; ideology is usually promoted by the **hegemonic** culture hides and justifies things which go against that culture; for example, a racist ideology might make people ignore racism or (if they can't ignore it) view racism as justified

Interactionism: a sociological Perspective that adopts a micro (small scale) approach; believes in understand individual motives and perceptions, often through examining how people play social roles or internalise **labels**

Intersectional: A 21st century approach to Sociology which focuses on how different identities combine to create privilege or oppression

Labelling Theory: an **Interactionist** explanation of deviance due to social labels with master status that are internalised, producing a self-fulfilling prophecy, according to **Becker (1963)**

Latent function: The hidden effects of social institutions, that befit society without us noticing

Manifest function: The obvious effects of social institutions, that benefit society in ways we all recognise

Marxism: a sociological Perspective that identifies conflict between social classes; believes in a **ruling class** exploiting a **working class**, both through violet force and **ruling class ideology**

Mass Media: technological forms of communication that can reach millions (or billions of people); traditionally radio, TV, film and print but now including the digital media, such as websites, social media, text messaging and mobile phones

Meritocracy: A system that rewards talent and effort with social advancement; specifically, the idea that education recognises and gives qualifications to the most intelligent people, assigning them to the most important jobs with the biggest rewards. The opposite is **social reproduction**.

Meta-Narrative: a 'Big Story' or grand philosophy that offers an explanation for everything (e.g. Christianity, Marxism, science, democracy) which is impossible to accept for **Postmodernists**

Moral Panic: process where the Media identifies a group as a threat, exaggerates its importance, arouses public concern and brings about new policies and social change

Neo-Marxism: several new interpretations of **Marxism** that emerged in the 1970s and became mainstream in the 1990s, incorporating elements of **Interactionism** to Marxist thought

New Right: a sociological Perspective that proposes we are experience social collapse brought on by a welfare culture that rewards worklessness and deviance in the **Underclass**

Norms: ways of behaving seen as acceptable or expected in society; based on underlying **values**

Patriarchy: The way society is structured around the interests of males, giving status to masculine behaviour and values and systematically subordinating women; masculine **hegemony** in society

Postmodernism: a sociological Perspective that proposes we are living in a new phase of social development, characterised by media saturation, diversity, choice, fluidity and fragmentation

Ruling class: A **hegemonic** group in society that controls the wealth and power, supported by an ideology that either hides or justifies their influence; Marx termed the ruling class 'the bourgeoisie' but **Neo-Marxists** often term it the **Hegemony**

Ruling class ideology: a set of beliefs promoted by the ruling class to preserve their power over the working class; ideology hides the injustice in society and justifies it when it cannot hide it

Semiology: technique for interpreting symbolic or coded behaviour to reveal its sociological meaning, popular with **Neo-Marxists**

Social class: A system for separating people based on their economic position (wealth, income, status); originally a split between the **ruling class** and **working class**, but later admitting of a middle class in between and now many more classes

Socialisation: The process of acquiring norms and values due to upbringing (primary socialisation) and education/experience (secondary socialisation)

Social reproduction: the opposite of **Meritocracy**; the idea that social divisions are reproduced each generation despite the education people receive

Social solidity: The experience of 'belonging' in society, linked to **value consensus**; it is the opposite of **anomie**

Spectacular Youth Subculture: several very visible and socially shocking youth subcultures that appeared in the 1950s, '60s and '70s; studied by the **CCS**

Subculture: a group within society that shares some of the **norms and values** of mainstream society but also has distinctive norms and values of its own

Transgression: Behaviour that goes against the rules or laws; similar to **deviance**

Underclass: term used by the **New Right** for a class below the working class, characterised by single mothers on benefits, poorly socialised children and irresponsible, workless and crime-prone adult males

Value consensus: The set of norms and values around which there is (supposedly) broad agreement in society; includes views on history, religion, morality, lifestyle and wealth

Values: powerful ideas shared by people in a culture about what is right and desirable and what is shameful or wrong; often expressed in behaviour as **norms**

Western culture: the culture of the UK, European countries, North America and Australia, that emerged out of the shared experience of Christianity, the Industrial Revolution and the development of democracy; an important part of **Global Culture**; responsible for developing Capitalism

White collar crime: crime carried out by powerful people in the course of doing their respectable jobs; includes embezzling money, tax fraud, breaking health & safety regulations and environmental pollution.

Working class: The majority group in society that is systematically excluded from access to wealth and power; controlled by **ideology** and the threat of force by the **ruling class**; Marx terms the working class 'the proletariat.'

ABOUT THE AUTHOR

Jonathan Rowe is a teacher of Religious Studies, Psychology and Sociology at Spalding Grammar School and he creates and maintains **www.psychologywizard.net** and the **www.philosophydungeon.weebly.com** site for Edexcel A-Level Religious Studies. He has worked as an examiner for various Exam Boards but is not affiliated with OCR. This series of books grew out of the resources he created for his students. Jonathan also writes novels and creates resources for his hobby of fantasy wargaming. He likes warm beer and smooth jazz.

Printed in Great Britain
by Amazon